ROBERT OF ARBRISSEL

ROBERT OF ARBRISSEL
A Medieval Religious Life

*Documents translated and annotated
by Bruce L. Venarde*

The Catholic University of America Press
Washington, D.C.

Printed in the United States of America

The paper used in this publication meets the minimum requirements of
American National Standards for Information Science—Permanence of
Paper for Printed Library materials, ANSI Z39.48-1984.
∞

Library of Congress Cataloging-in-Publication Data

Robert of Arbrissel : a medieval religious life / documents translated
and annotated by Bruce L. Venarde.
   p.   cm. — (Medieval texts in translation)
Includes bibliographical references and index.
ISBN 0-8132-1354-1 (pbk. : alk. paper)
   1. Robert, of Arbrissel, ca. 1045–1117.   2. Catholic Church—France—
Clergy—Biography.   3. Robert, of Arbrissel, ca. 1045–1117—Correspondence.   4. Catholic Church—France—Clergy—Correspondence.
5. Abbaye de Fontevrault—Charters.   I. Robert, of Arbrissel, ca.
1045–1117.   II. Venarde, Bruce L., 1962–   III. Series.
BX4705.R578 R636 2004
271'.79—dc21

                                                      2002154381

For Jack and Dell Venarde

CONTENTS

ACKNOWLEDGMENTS

For a small book, this one has a big support system. Those who have encouraged the idea and helped along the way include Renate Blumenfeld-Kosinski, Janelle Greenberg, Maureen Miller, Thomas Noble, Barbara Rosenwein, Susan Sherman, Dell Venarde, and Jack Venarde.

For financial assistance I am very grateful to the Catholic University of America Press and David McGonagle, and to three units at the University of Pittsburgh: the Department of Classics and its chair, Edwin Floyd; the Department of History and its chair, G. Reid Andrews; and the Center for West European Studies and its director, Alberta Sbragia. Professor Andrews also very kindly arranged for me to have a semester away from teaching to facilitate completion of the manuscript. Karen Green generously shared translations with me; careful and capable translation review, saving me from small and not-so-small errors, has been provided by Susan Dudash, Sr. Maria Kiely (who also alerted me to a number of biblical and patristic references), and David Nelson. I appreciate the assistance of patient and efficient librarians at the Andover and Widener Libraries of Harvard University and Hillman Library at the University of Pittsburgh, especially Jerry Heverly. As always, I am lucky to have Jack Eckert as an in-house reference specialist and for a lot of other reasons.

I wish I could blame any of these people for the imperfections of what follows. Baudri of Dol protested his inadequacy to write about Robert of Arbrissel on the grounds of poor prose style, other urgent business in an uncultured environment, lack of information, advanced age, indolence, and chronically sinful ways. I have only some of these excuses for my mistakes. This book is for my father, born the day Robert of Arbrissel died and more like him than he knows, and for my mother, who has long shared my fascination with Robert.

CHRONOLOGY OF ROBERT OF ARBRISSEL'S LIFE

ca. 1045
Robert born in the village of Arbrissel in southeastern Brittany

1076
Robert participates in the election of Sylvester de la Guerche as bishop of Rennes

1080s
Robert a student in Paris

1089–1093
Robert serves as archpriest of Rennes at the invitation of Bishop Sylvester

1093–1095
Robert resumes studies in Angers

1095
Robert retires to the forest of Craon, not far from his birthplace, where he soon attracts a crowd of disciples

1096
February 10th: Robert preaches in Angers at the request of Pope Urban II

February 11th: Formal recognition of Robert's followers in the forest of Craon as the canonical community of La Roë

Robert begins his career as errant evangelist, dividing his time between La Roë and the road

ca. 1098

Robert leaves La Roë permanently for full-time preaching

Marbode of Rennes writes a letter sharply critical of Robert's failure to
supervise those his preaching has inspired, especially women

1100

November: Robert attends an ecclesiastical council in Poitiers

1101

Robert settles his followers at Fontevraud

ca. 1103

Robert, having seen to the beginnings of a permanent monastic settlement at Fontevraud, names two female superiors and goes back to
errant preaching

ca. 1103–1115

Robert tours western and central France preaching and founding new
monasteries for his followers

1106

Fontevraud is taken under papal and episcopal protection in letters from
Bishop Peter II of Poitiers and Pope Pascal II

ca. 1107

Abbot Geoffrey of Vendôme criticizes Robert's relations with his female
followers

1109

Robert commends the monasteries he has founded in the diocese of
Poitiers to the care of Bishop Peter II

Robert writes an exhortation to Countess Ermengarde of Brittany

1115

July 11th: Robert gives properties in Cadouin to Gerald of Sales

September: Robert assembles a council of clerics to discuss appoint-
ment of an abbess for Fontevraud

October 28th: Robert appoints Petronilla of Chemillé as the first abbess
of Fontevraud

Late October–November: Robert asks Bishop Gerard of Angoulême, a papal legate, to confirm the election of Abbess Petronilla. Gerard does so and also arranges for notice to be sent from Pope Pascal II in Rome.

Robert issues rules of conduct for religious women and men at Fontevraud

December: Robert, on the road again, settles a dispute between the monks of Bonneval and the bishop of Chartres

December 25th: Robert celebrates Christmas at the monastery of Hautes-Bruyères

1116

January: Robert returns to Chartres to settle troubles between the count and the cathedral clergy, then visits Count William of Nevers in prison at Blois

End of January/beginning of February: Robert travels to Orsan

Mid-February: Robert goes to Déols

February 18th: Robert leaves Déols for Graçay

February 19th: After a night at Graçay, Robert says he is about to die and asks to be carried back to Orsan. On the way he spends the night at Issoudun

February 20th: Robert arrives at Orsan in the evening

February 21st–24th: Anticipating death, Robert receives communion every day

February 22nd: Robert receives the sacrament of extreme unction. Archbishop Leger of Bourges, Abbess Petronilla, and numerous local lords gather at Orsan

February 23rd: Robert asks Archbishop Leger and Prioress Agnes of Orsan to see to it that his body is returned to Fontevraud for burial

February 24th: Robert makes the same request of Alard, a founder of Orsan

February 25th: Robert dies in the evening; his body, transferred to the nuns' cloister, is taken from there by Archbishop Leger's entourage

February 26th: Robert's body is dressed and a coffin made

February 27th: Archbishop Leger, in an assembly of laity and clergy, decides to keep Robert's body at Orsan. Abbess Petronilla strongly objects

February 28th: The nuns make a penitential procession to protest the archbishop's decision

February 29th: Archbishop Leger decides to let Robert's body be returned to Fontevraud

March 1st: Abbess Petronilla and her party begin the journey back to Fontevraud

March 5th: Robert's body arrives at Fontevraud late in the evening and lies in state in the Great Monastery

March 6th: Robert's body is taken to Saint-Lazare, then the Madeleine, where it stays for the night

March 7th: After public display in front of Fontevraud's main church, Robert's body is buried by the high altar amid a crowd of distinguished clergy and laity

ca. 1118–1120
Composition of the two *vitae*, the first by Baudri of Dol, the second by Robert's chaplain, Andreas

1119
September 15th: Pope Calixtus II consecrates the abbey church of Fontevraud

1149
Death of Abbess Petronilla of Chemillé. By this time Fontevraud has more than fifty daughter houses in France and Aragon; several more, including three in England, are established in the following decades

INTRODUCTION: ROBERT OF ARBRISSEL'S WORLD

Count Fulk V of Anjou, the future king of Jerusalem, called his preaching a thunderclap of holy exhortation that lit up the whole Church with its eloquence. Contemporary churchmen feared he was a danger to his own soul and the souls of his female followers. The teacher and theologian Peter Abelard called him "that outstanding herald of Christ."[1] Since his appearance into public view 900 years ago, Robert of Arbrissel (ca. 1045–1116) has attracted a range of opinions and interpretations. Robert was an ordained Catholic priest, but he is hard to label because he had various missions, and what we might call several different careers, from the 1070s to his death. At various times parish priest, longtime student, bishop's aide and archpriest in his native Brittany, hermit, preacher who crisscrossed western France for two decades, and founder of monasteries where men and women joined in lives of prayer and contemplation, Robert remains a figure about whom experts cannot agree. Feminist or proto-feminist? Champion of the downtrodden? Reformer, rebel, borderline heretic, or simply a guilt-ridden medieval Christian acting out his spiritual pain? This book gathers for the first time materials written during or shortly after Robert of Arbrissel's lifetime. Readers can use them to come to their own conclusions about this controversial and restless preacher and pastor.[2]

Economy, Society, Power, and Gender

To begin to understand Robert of Arbrissel requires some familiarity with his world, northwestern France in the eleventh and early twelfth centuries.[3] This was, first, a largely rural society. Western France, the central part of Europe bordering the Atlantic Ocean, is at one end of a great fertile agricultural plain that stretches across northern Europe eastward to Russia. Besides rich soil, the region is blessed with moderate climate and abundant rainfall, and well drained by dozens of streams and rivers. Over several centuries, the peasant majority, those who tilled the soil to support themselves and a much smaller elite group, had learned to use this tremendous natural resource with considerable efficiency. Peasants improved techniques for exploiting animal power and the earth's self-rejuvenating qualities in crop rotation. Such changes did not by any means end poverty and desperation; in the eleventh century and beyond, famine still struck regularly. A year or two of crop failure owing to bad weather or disease could have devastating effects. Nonetheless, by 1000 A.D., European population had begun to grow steadily after centuries of virtual stagnation. More people produced and required more food. The eleventh and twelfth centuries were a time of extension of land available for the grain crops that were the basis of the European diet. Peasants cleared forests and drained swamps, even reclaimed tidal areas from the sea, immensely increasing the acreage of arable land. In some of the regions Robert of Arbrissel traversed, the amount of land under the plow reached its sustainable maximum in the twelfth century, and the total size and distribution of farmland remains much the same today.

Population growth was gradual and did not outpace agricultural expansion, making both qualitative and quantitative social change possible. Per capita income was on the rise, albeit so gradually that few people would have perceived it. But they would have noticed the development of cities, where nonagricultural laborers could live and work. Very slowly, manufacture and trade were becoming significant sectors of the European economy. Urban life in Europe had largely disappeared with the Roman Empire, and even in Robert of Arbrissel's day, probably only four cities in the northwestern French districts where he spent most of his time—Angers, Poitiers, Tours, and Rennes—had populations of more than a few thousand. But cities, for centuries past little more than the homes of the regional chief priests called bishops, were now serving as centers of economic vitality, intellectual ferment, and secular as well as ecclesiastical power. Robert spent some years in Paris as a student, preached before the pope in the Loire Valley town of Angers, and traveled to the cities of Rouen (near the English Channel) and Agen (in southwestern France). For much of his life, Robert moved back and forth between urban and rural environments, although his choice of venue was the latter. In Robert's day and for long after, the vast majority of Europeans continued to live in the countryside, in communities of only a few dozen or a few score.

The peasant majority and the small if growing number of city dwellers were not the only, or even the primary, beneficiaries of rural economic and demographic expansion. Most rural dwellers— some 90–95 percent of the population of Europe in Robert's lifetime—were not free farmers who owned the land they worked. Instead, they were serfs, the tenants and charges of their overlords, the military and ecclesiastical ruling class. Lords ranged in status and might from small proprietors who controlled only a few dozen acres to mighty titled nobles. Religious institutions were also great landlords, in control of perhaps a third of all cultivated land in northern France by the end of the twelfth century. Serfs owed rent (in money, goods, or a combination) and often labor services, a certain number of days a year working the estate of their lords. Peasants were obliged to donate a tenth of their produce to the Church: the tithe. Other occasional payments to various officials were also typical. This heavily burdened peasantry was a largely illiterate majority whose lives we know only indirectly. They supported the minority lordly society about which we are much better informed and among whom Robert of Arbrissel spent much of his time.

The medieval elite was a warrior class. Fighting was the primary occupation of most of its male members. Ambitious warrior nobles great and small were in constant competition with each other and made a dizzying array of ever shifting alliances. The result was highly decentralized political power, perhaps nowhere more so than in western Continental Europe. Most people understood and experienced power only locally, according to who had the rights to tax and hold court in a given place. Law was often no more than the will of the lord nearby. There were kings of West Frankland, coming to be known as "France," but they were not, during Robert's lifetime, very influential figures outside the estates they controlled around Paris. King Philip I (1060–1108) made no attempt at all to assert his authority in southern France; Abbot Geoffrey of Vendôme, who wrote scores of letters, including one to Robert translated below, addressed popes in distant Rome but never in all his voluminous correspondence so much as *mentioned* the king of France, whose capital of Paris was only 200 kilometers from Geoffrey's monastery. Among the most effective lords in France were the counts of Anjou in their capital city of Angers, but in Robert's time, they struggled to maintain their authority across a large region filled with aspiring and aggressive armed men. In short, localism was a key trait of Robert's world.

Although most lords were warriors, some joined the Church as monks, withdrawing to communities whose purpose was prayer for all of Christian society. Others became officials in the so-called secular church, those institutions directly involved with the spiritual care of individual lay Christians. In this society, the most powerful religious *and* secular officers came from the same families and thus, despite the apparent differences in their ways of life, were informed by similar values and ideals. Indeed, pious nobles were great patrons of religious people and their institutions. The foundation and patronage of monasteries, in particular, was a nonmilitary arena of competition between propertied families, a fact of which Robert took advantage when he founded permanent settlements for his followers.

This was largely a man's world. A woman served her class as the wife and mother of new warriors and clerics or as a nun, the only Christian profession open to women. Many women also acted as secular and ecclesiastical leaders, diplomats, landlords, and patrons of religion and the arts.[4] However, lordly families in the eleventh and twelfth centuries began to define themselves in terms of descent down male lines, called patrilineage. Female ancestry came to matter less, with women instead serving to unite male descent groups; children were heirs to the property and titles of their male ancestors. With patrilineage came preference for primogeniture: passing along a family's property intact to the eldest male child. Females could and often did inherit, but not all elite women were possessors of land and goods to do with what they pleased. Only in the absence of brothers would a woman stand to inherit the bulk of a family estate, and such heiresses were vigorously pursued by potential husbands.[5] Marriage was a matter of alliance between families rather than a joining of individuals that reflected mutual yearning. Thus both men and women often married people they barely knew. Furthermore, males of the propertied class were likely to postpone marriage until they could be assured of their fortune, so they were frequently much older than their brides. This meant that women who survived childbirth were likely to become widows. In Robert's time, society included a large number of widows. It is clear that his message and personality were especially powerful for widows and unhappily married wives.

Religion and the Church

The desire to dominate was common among Europe's ruling class, its warrior nobles and their churchly sons, brothers, uncles, nephews, and cousins. Since the late tenth century, bishops and other religious officials in Western Europe had legislated against armed violence harmful to the poor and powerless, thereby creating a movement known as the Peace of God.[6] Churchmen desired to attain some measure of leadership over the society with whose spiritual care they were charged, a world in which arbitrary violence and the lawlessness that accompanied political decentralization seemed at times to threaten anarchy. In the eleventh century, assemblies of the Peace of God, attended by crowds of enthusiastic laypeople mighty and humble, resulted in detailed written prescriptions against various social ills. By 1050, the impulse to religious and social change was centered in Rome. The papacy, for most of the previous millennium more a symbolic than a real center of power and command in the Catholic Church, began to assert its authority in numerous ways. The reformers in Rome first addressed what they saw as the moral and spiritual inadequacies of the European clergy, from ill-educated peasant priests to corrupt high officials who had obtained their jobs through gifts to powerful warriors—usually their relatives. Besides taking aim at the trade in spiritual offices and the indirect domination of the Church by the masters of the world that such trade implied, the newly invigorated papacy also prohibited the marriage of clergy, until then a practice typical of the clerical rank-and-file and not unknown among the higher clergy, including a dynasty of eleventh-century bishops in Robert's native Brittany.

The reinvigorated papacy's aim was the division of Christian society into two distinct realms: sacred and profane, ecclesiastical and secular. Such a conceptual divide is familiar to us. But the idea was novel, even revolutionary, in the eleventh century. The program as a whole is often called "Gregorian Reform" after Pope Gregory

VII (1073–1085), one of its most vigorous proponents. Gregory and his successors took on kings and emperors with papal claim to spiritual lordship over all Christendom and insistence that boundaries between matters religious and mundane be carefully observed. In the process, they made the papacy the spiritual and practical head of the Catholic Church, now truly the Roman Church.

These changes took generations to achieve, and whether the new separatist ideology would prevail was very much in question during Robert of Arbrissel's lifetime. Many people, both laity and clergy, objected to any change in what they understood to be venerable, customary practices of religious and social organization. Robert's activities were heavily influenced by these debates. He was a student in Paris during the reign of Pope Gregory VII, and subsequently worked in his native Brittany to enforce some of the new ideas about how clergy should behave. In 1096 Robert was asked to preach by Pope Urban II (1088–1099), who expanded on Gregory VII's programs by calling on Europe's warring elites to focus their aggression in holy war, the series of conflicts known as the Crusades. At the same time, the demand for clerical celibacy implied strict separation of men and women, a vision of religious life and work Robert did not share. Some women who followed him were probably onetime clerical wives or concubines, dislocated from their old lives by enforcement of the new ideas of sexual purity and gender separatism. Robert roused both admiration and criticism by accepting some, but not all, of the reform program. He counseled obedience to church officials—including their new claims to supervision of marriage and divorce—but also criticized clerical morals. He championed clerical celibacy, but his pastoral mission to women and the mingling of the sexes in communities of his followers challenged the prevailing agenda of gender apartheid and the mistrust of women common to many Christian reformers of his day.

Robert's religious vision, then, both conformed to and diverged from the program formulated in Rome. The accomplishment for which Robert is best remembered, however, was in the mainstream: the foundation of regular religious communities, that is, those organized according to a written rule (*regula* in Latin). The band of hermits who had gathered around Robert in southeastern Brittany became a religious house called La Roë in 1096. After he left La Roë for full-time preaching, Robert was stung by criticism that he did not take appropriate care of his followers. In 1101 Robert established a group of these devotees at a place called Fontevraud, just south of the Loire River where the borders of three regions of western France—Anjou, Poitou, and Touraine—coincided. Robert's original intentions for this mixed community of women and men in pursuit of spiritual excellence are unclear. But Fontevraud soon evolved into a traditional monastic house for women (albeit with resident male brothers as aides). Satellite or daughter houses of Fontevraud multiplied in the years before and after Robert's death. Robert's communities, which he founded with the cooperation of bishops and landowning elites, were part of a pan-European enthusiasm for religious foundations in the late eleventh and twelfth centuries. Here again, Robert shared in the new religious impulses—and competition for spiritual excellence—characteristic of his age.[7] When Robert was buried at Fontevraud, only fifteen years after its foundation, the abbey and its daughter houses were well on the way to becoming what they remained for seven centuries: the largest and wealthiest order of monasteries for women in Roman Catholic Europe.

Despite the lasting legacy of the Order of Fontevraud, Robert did not identify himself solely as a founder of monasteries. Instead, preaching occupied most of the last twenty years of his life. Robert's style of evangelism, aimed at all sorts and conditions of Christians, was not a major concern of the church leaders of his day. Most preaching of the era was in Latin, the common language of the educated elite, and took place behind monastery walls or in great city churches. For the rural majority, such religious instruction as there was long remained in the hands of parish priests.

Priests were responsible primarily for the Latin liturgy, prayer services and rituals like baptism and the Mass. Most churchgoers were spectators rather than meaningful participants in services in Latin, a language they did not know, and most lay Christians, even elite ones, probably heard sermons only occasionally. Many officials thought public preaching was or should be the monopoly of bishops. Some bishops, including Hildebert of Le Mans, to whom is attributed the poetic remembrance of Robert of Arbrissel translated below, were known for their ability to preach in the spoken language of the people. However, a bishop's region, called his diocese, was usually of such a size that he could not, even if he had wanted to, preach everywhere regularly. Ambitious preaching campaigns emerged organically, as they did in northern and western France with Robert and others like him (on whom see below).[8]

Movements like the Peace of God showed that many ordinary medieval Christians, both lords and peasants, responded with great enthusiasm to meaningful spiritual messages despite their lack of much in the way of religious instruction. Preaching was hardly the only means of religious education. People of all ranks enjoyed religious holidays, celebrations of events and people in Christian history. Churches were decorated, often heavily so, with instructive painting and sculptures, in particular carvings of the Virgin Mary and the infant Jesus or crucifixes. In larger churches, dramas illustrating biblical stories, sometimes accompanied by music, also had didactic intentions. But effective preaching like Robert's, which delivered a message that seemed personally relevant to listeners, was rare—a side-effect, at best, of the concerns of reformers in Robert's era. Robert's allies and critics agreed that his words were forceful and that his sermons influenced a diverse cross-section of his society, from popes to peasants. Much of Robert's notoriety rested on his ability to satisfy the spiritual yearning of a diverse audience. In his own view, Robert was serving his faith in a rather different way than the Christian officials of his day, the popes and bishops and abbots who focused on purity and order as the means toward universal salvation. Robert chose instead to speak to individual hearts and minds.

Whatever his deviation from others' visions of spiritual purity and excellence, Robert shared in the reformers' religious culture—and the culture of the men whose writings about him are translated in this book—because he had been educated the same way. Before the origins of universities in the twelfth century, monasteries and cathedral schools were the two fora for Christian Latin education. Robert studied at cathedral schools in Paris and Angers; his critic Marbode of Rennes was the director of studies at Angers, and Abbot Geoffrey of Vendôme also studied there. Robert's biographer Baudri of Dol was the product of monastic education, as was, most likely, the Brother Andreas of Fontevraud who also wrote extensively about Robert. Whether in monasteries or cathedral schools, students learned the traditional seven liberal arts. First came the *trivium* of grammar, rhetoric, and logic—that is, sophisticated reading of a variety of Latin texts, effective writing and speaking, and coherent reasoning. There followed the *quadrivium* of music, astronomy, arithmetic, and geometry. Advanced subjects included medicine, in its infancy as a course of study in Robert's time; law, revived in the wake of the Gregorian Reform; and theology, or religious philosophy and speculation. Robert's education seems to have included some study of canon (church) law, which he may have learned at Angers, since both Marbode and Geoffrey had some familiarity with the subject; he certainly studied theology. But it was mastery of the *trivium* that propelled Robert's career as preacher of God's Word.

Robert and His Circle

It was in this environment—vital, competitive, energetic, and filled with a variety of competing ideas and visions—that Robert of Arbrissel lived and worked. Despite Robert's reputation for eccentricity, his activities were not unique and he was never an isolated figure. When Robert retired to live as a hermit in 1095, he was taking part in a widespread contemporary enthusiasm for spiritual life in solitude.[9] "Solitude" in this case did not mean utterly solitary life; like many who chose to live in sparsely populated areas, Robert started with a companion and soon attracted more. Many hermits interspersed life in the wilderness with more active missions, including preaching. The urge to live in the wilderness appears to have reached its height in France during Robert's lifetime. Two other hermit-preachers who also ended up founding monastic houses were Robert's friends Bernard of Tiron and Vitalis of Savigny.[10] One of Robert's companions from his hermit days was Gerald of Sales, to whom Robert transferred some properties, a donation recorded in a document translated in this book.

Robert benefited during much of his career from the patronage of ecclesiastical officials. His student days in Paris ended when Bishop Sylvester of Rennes called on him for aid in governing Robert's native diocese as archpriest. No less a figure than Pope Urban II invited him to preach at a ceremony in Angers in 1096. Abbot Geoffrey of Vendôme wrote a highly critical letter to Robert but also established special spiritual bonds between Fontevraud and his own monastery. Fellow preacher Bishop Hildebert of Le Mans was an ally and poetic commemorator of Robert; Robert's funeral oration was delivered by Archbishop Leger of Bourges in an assembly that included many other prelates. But Robert's most important clerical patron was Bishop Peter II of Poitiers. It was almost certainly Peter who arranged for Robert to settle some of his followers at Fontevraud in 1101. The documents in this book show that, until he died shortly before Robert, the bishop continued to support and protect him. Although Robert held an ecclesiastical title only during his time as archpriest of Rennes in 1089–1093, he was surrounded by churchmen from his birth as the son of a village priest to his burial.

Robert was also surrounded by laypeople who were his disciples and patrons, from the king of France to the lepers and desperate poor who composed some of the original community at Fontevraud. To live independently of institutions and essentially homeless, as Robert did for the last twenty years of his life, required the charity and protection of the mighty in the decentralized society of northwestern France. For those who traveled frequently or lived in isolation, this was particularly important. Robert's fellow hermit-preacher Bernard of Tiron was harassed by pirates while pursuing solitude on islands off the coast of Brittany; highway robbers attacked Robert himself only a few weeks before he died. While he was a hermit, Robert attracted the protection and generosity of nearby lords, who continued their patronage as Robert's little band of hermits evolved into the traditional religious house of La Roë. Among the earliest supporters of Fontevraud were local lords. Hautes-Bruyères, the daughter house of Fontevraud where Robert spent his last Christmas, was built with the cooperation of King Louis VII (1108–1137). At the other end of the social scale were humble people (who also contributed to the nascent community at Fontevraud) and outcasts like prostitutes and lepers to whom Robert's message was attractive. Robert's patrons, disciples, and colleagues included a large number of women, apparently the majority among his followers. Robert's extremely close relations with them were a cause for alarm in his lifetime and long after. It is fitting, then, that the only surviving example of spiritual direction from Robert's pen is addressed to a woman, Countess Ermengarde of Brittany, the sister of his benefactor Count Fulk V of Anjou.

Reading Robert

This book translates a variety of medieval documents concerning Robert of Arbrissel and his activities, written in Latin either during his lifetime or soon after his death.[11] Like every text, from a menu to a tax form, medieval sources have to be read carefully. In these materials about Robert, questions about the genre, authorial intent, audience, and purpose(s) of each text are all important. It is vital to remember that these were Latin texts, available to the small minority of people in Robert's world who had been educated. The two longest documents, extended accounts of Robert's actions by Bishop Baudri of Dol and Brother Andreas of Fontevraud, belong to the literary tradition of hagiography, which means "writing about holy people." Hagiography, a vast body of medieval literature, concerns the activities of holy people, men and women understood by faithful Christians to have led lives that made them special in heaven, with privileged access to God.[12] For many centuries, the designation of any one such holy person as a saint was a more or less spontaneous process, but in the twelfth century, prescribed procedures were emerging that gave the papacy the final say on canonization, formal elevation to saintly status. That evolution from localized and spontaneous recognition to authoritarian and procedural designation was taking place during Robert's lifetime. The written record was central to it: written evidence became, as it has remained, key to the canonization process. Indeed, one reason to write about Robert's activities was in view of an attempt to have him declared a saint (which, as we shall see, never succeeded). Narratives about holy people and their activities are called *vitae*, or "lives," so I call what Baudri and Andreas each wrote a *vita*. Such writings come in many forms and with many themes, but two things about hagiographical writing in the eleventh and twelfth centuries are especially important. First, traditionally *vitae* had been written about people long dead, but in the second millennium authors began to write routinely about contemporaries, even people they knew. Secondly, these new *vitae* continued to be heavily influenced by older writing on saints. The single most important model in the Latin West was the account of St. Martin of Tours (d. 397) by Sulpicius Severus. Martin, a soldier, a monk, a missionary to pagans, and finally a charismatic bishop, was in his conduct and appeal much like Robert of Arbrissel, a fact not lost on Brother Andreas.[13] The hagiographical dossier on Robert, then, draws on old and new traditions.

There are also three letters here, two addressed to Robert and one written by him. Medieval letters were not the same as modern private correspondence, since it was the usual assumption that there would be multiple readers. Letters were testimonies, written with care. Both of the letters to Robert, from Marbode of Rennes and Geoffrey of Vendôme, are highly critical rebukes and even warnings to an unusual spiritual brother. Both men chose their words and arranged their thoughts carefully, reflecting both the training in the *trivium* they shared with Robert and their view of right Christian order. Robert's letter is pastoral advice to Countess Ermengarde, offering her a design for piety she could express amid the cares of busy court life; although written with its recipient's needs in mind, it was probably still not meant to be completely private. Robert also wrote short instructions for the women and men of Fontevraud. These were explicitly written for a group. Like letters, medieval poetry was meant for single readers as well as assemblies of listeners. The poem of tribute in Robert's honor probably composed by Bishop Hildebert of Le Mans should be considered as a text designed for individual and collective reading.

Finally, several documents in this book belong to the genre of charter. A charter is technically anything written down, usually the record of an important event. For most of the early medieval period (ca. 500–1000 A.D.), written records are scarce; historians know much more about medieval society after the tenth century than before, largely because so much more was committed to writing later. Records came to substitute for individual memories.[14] The charters in this book concern the transfer of property or its supervision, but each also tells something about Robert, those around him, and the times in which he lived.

This collection, then, is a mixture of several kinds of medieval writings united by their depiction of Robert of Arbrissel.[15] I have chosen to put the two *vitae* first, since they provide the most extensive descriptions of Robert's activities. Then follow documents written by Robert himself: his letter to Ermengarde, two charters, and the statutes for Fontevraud. Next come the letters of Marbode of Rennes and Geoffrey of Vendôme, written about ten years apart but having in common their concern that Robert's allure was leading his followers astray and that his behavior was outside the bounds of propriety—if not decency. The collection ends with four short documents that tell a little more about Robert's life and death.

Nearly all these materials were written over the course of about twenty years, ca. 1098–ca. 1120. What follows is a compilation of contemporary records about Robert of Arbrissel—his actions, his character, and his influence on those around him. They are organized to produce a detailed and complex view, an intimate look at one man's life, experiences, and beliefs.[16] I hope readers will learn as much puzzling over the unique Robert of Arbrissel as I do.

NOTES ON TRANSLATION

Any translation is necessarily an interpretation, so it seems wise to explain a few of my choices.

In medieval Latin, authors sometimes used the first person plural to refer to themselves. I have retained "I" and "we" literally. The rich word *religio* I have usually simply translated "religion"; *religio* and its cognates have a range of meanings, referring to institutional and spiritual manifestations of faith, and "religion" seems the best way to cover a number of its implications. On occasion, I have simplified extremely complex sentences and toned down rhetorical flourishes that were standard in medieval Latin writing but would read like pomposity in a modern English translation. However, I have retained many stylistic echoes of the classical Latin texts in which these authors were steeped.

With biblical references, quotations from the Vulgate (the Latin Bible of the Middle Ages) are italicized. As text reference I used one standard version, the Clementine Vulgate. However, there is no single text that can claim absolute authority as *the* Vulgate, which exists in numerous medieval manuscripts and scholarly editions that differ from one another. So readers should be aware that it is not possible to be absolutely certain when authors were quoting rather than rephrasing. Italicization, then, is no more than an indication of likely direct quotation from the Bible or Bibles known to the authors. I retain as quotations instances where words have been transposed but not changed or those in which a word like *enim*, which has no effect on the meaning of the sentence, has been added or omitted. In the section of Andreas's *vita* transmitted only in French translation, numerous Vulgate passages were retained by the translator in Latin; these, too, are italicized. Other bracketed notes signal strong verbal echoes to the Bible: near-quotations, paraphrases, or allusions. Since it would be anachronistic and deceptive to rely on any one English version in translating biblical passages, I have generally translated according to context, although some of the language will be familiar to those who know modern English-language versions.

Section numbering is that of the printed editions, with the exception of Robert's letter to Ermengarde, which I have divided into sections for ease of reference.

ABBREVIATIONS

CCCM   *Corpus christianorum. Continuatio medievalis.* Turnhout, 1966–

CCSL   *Corpus christianorum. Series latina.* Turnhout, 1953–

CSEL   *Corpus scriptorum ecclesiasticorum latinorum.* Vienna, 1866–

PL   *Patrologia cursus completus. Series latina.* Edited by J.-P. Migne. 221 volumes. Paris, 1844–1864

SC   *Sources chrétiennes.* Paris, 1941–

Note:
Because Migne's *Patrologia* is the most readily available collection of medieval Latin sources, I have cited it whenever possible. However, many of the text editions Migne used in his massive compilation have been superceded by modern scholarship. The four other series listed above contain many new editions and I cite them in the notes in addition to the PL. The PL is now accessible in an electronic version in many research libraries; the contents of the CCCM, CCSL, CSEL, and SC volumes, as well as many other Latin texts, are available on CD-ROM under the title *Library of Latin Texts* (older editions entitled *CETEDOC Library of Christian Latin Texts*).

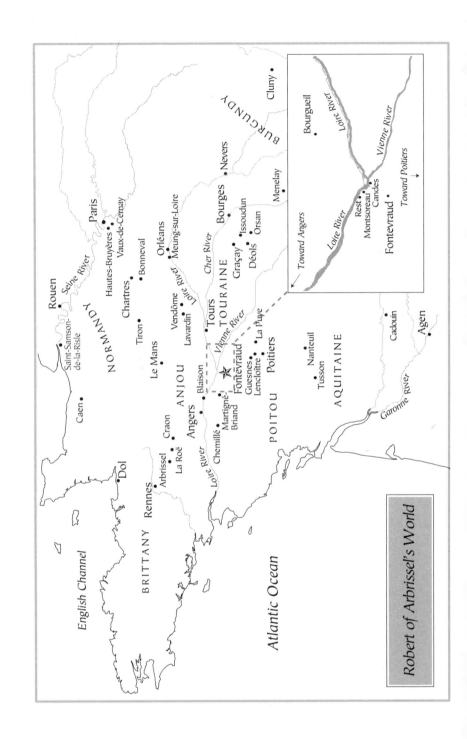

Robert of Arbrissel's World

ROBERT OF ARBRISSEL

BAUDRI OF DOL, *FIRST LIFE OF ROBERT OF ARBRISSEL* (CA. 1118)

Baudri of Dol, so called for the city over which he presided as bishop in the last decades of his life, was born around 1046, making him a contemporary of Robert of Arbrissel. The trajectory of his life, though, was much different and far more characteristic of the age. Baudri, whose family is unknown, came from Meung-sur-Loire, a village on the Loire not far from Orléans. All that is certain about his education is what Baudri himself wrote in a heart-rending poem lamenting the death of Hubert, his teacher at Meung. Tradition has it that Baudri also studied at the cathedral school of Angers under Marbode, who later wrote a letter highly critical of Robert of Arbrissel (translated below). Baudri and Marbode certainly knew each other, but there is no evidence Baudri studied at Angers. While a young man, Baudri entered the prosperous monastery of Bourgueil, on the north side of the Loire between Tours and Angers, and became its abbot in about 1079. Therefore he is often called Baudri of Bourgueil.

As abbot, Baudri worked to ensure adherence to the Benedictine Rule, the standard guide to Western Christian monastic life in the Middle Ages, named for its author, St. Benedict of Nursia (ca. 480–ca. 547). Baudri also built a library that reflected his intensive study of both Christian and pagan Roman texts. He became socially well connected, counting among his friends Adela, the countess of Blois, and her sister Cecilia, abbess of the monastery at Caen founded by their father, William the Conqueror. He was also an ally of Robert of Arbrissel, although perhaps not until Robert founded Fontevraud, only about fifteen kilometers from Bourgueil, in 1101. In 1107, Baudri was elected archbishop of Dol in Brittany and the next year went to Rome for personal induction by Pope Pascal II. Archbishop Baudri participated in ecclesiastical affairs of European scope, traveling to England (where he was so impressed by the pipe organ in the cathedral of Worcester that he wrote a poem about it) and around northern France. His last great journey was to Rome in 1123 for the First Lateran Council, a pan-European ecclesiastical conference presided over by Pope Calixtus II. Rather than return to Brittany, Baudri went to Normandy and settled on a small wooded property owned by the church of Dol called Saint-Samson-sur-la-Risle, just a few kilometers from the mouth of the Seine River. He died on January 7th, 1130, and was buried in the nearby nunnery of Préaux.

Baudri was a learned and prolific writer of prose and poetry. Wherever he got his education, it was thorough, since his writing reflects deep study of classical Latin writers, especially the orator and politician Cicero and the poets Vergil and Ovid. It is Ovid who most influenced Baudri's poetry. Over 250 poems survive, most of which Baudri appears to have written at Bourgueil, before his elevation to Dol. The most famous is a 1,368-verse letter-poem addressed to Countess Adela. It is a miniature encyclopedia in the form of an imagined description of Adela's palace with its wall paintings and tapestries illustrating sacred and secular history, mythology, astrology, astronomy, geography, philosophy, education in the seven liberal arts, and medicine. The idea for the poem was not original to Baudri, but its length and completeness were unprecedented; its contents were imitated and echoed in numerous Latin and French poems thereafter. Baudri also adapted his master Ovid by writing a dialogue between Paris and Helen, whose affair started the Trojan War of Greek myth, poetry, and drama. Other poems range in length from one line to several hundred, including other letter-poems, a lengthy treatment of legends from classical mythology with etymological and moral commentary, epitaphs, eulogies of people and places, numerous occasional pieces, and lyric, often playful and sometimes frankly erotic. Baudri's verse refers to fellow poets Hildebert of Le Mans (whose epitaph of Robert of Arbrissel is translated below) and Marbode. His poetic outlook is notably sunny, open, and optimistic; he regarded monastic life as the ideal setting for literary pursuits and as a writer positioned himself at the crossroads of pagan learning and Christian monastic traditions.

Most of Baudri's prose writing apparently dates to when he was archbishop (1107–1130). It reflects less classical models than the biblical teaching in which he, like the other authors in this book, was steeped. Baudri's best-known narrative is an account of the First Crusade. The archbishop never went to the East; what he called the *History of Jerusalem* is a revision in elevated (Ciceronian) style of a firsthand report written by a priest who had been in the Holy Land with the Crusader army. Baudri expanded that narrative and included a version of the speech given by Pope Urban II in 1095 that launched the Crusade. Other medieval authors, including the distinguished Norman historian Orderic Vitalis, worked from Baudri's version. Orderic apparently knew the aged Baudri, and wrote a sketch of his life calling the Bretons, his archepiscopal flock, savage and perverse (a characterization echoed by Baudri's comments in the *vita* of Robert of Arbrissel, section 2). Baudri also wrote *vitae* of long-dead saints. His biography of St. Samson, first bishop of Dol (501–565), reworked an earlier text; he also wrote on St. Hugh, archbishop of Rouen (d. 730), the city not far from where Baudri retired near the end of his life. Among his prose letters is a long account addressed to the monks of the Norman abbey of Fécamp, which includes some autobiographical detail on Baudri's travels as well as descriptions of the countryside surrounding Fécamp and the monastery itself.

Baudri doubtless knew Robert of Arbrissel, whose foundation and tomb, Fontevraud, was not far from Bourgueil; a friendship would account for the request by Abbess Petronilla that Baudri write a *vita* of Robert. Baudri's poetic output included nearly 100 epitaphs, poems lamenting the death of people ranging from archbishops to a female hermit to infants. This collection, along with other hagiographical works and the renown of Baudri's history of the First Crusade, may have encouraged Petronilla. Whatever the rationale, the request came shortly after Robert's death in 1116, when Baudri was based in Dol and busy with the affairs of his diocese and the European Church at large. The result was a *vita* precious to historians, since it gives the most detail of any document about the whole course of Robert's life. At the same time, it is brief, sometimes vague, and was not, most likely, what Petronilla would have liked as a memorial of the founder of her abbey and its numerous daughter houses.

Baudri begins with several paragraphs of what one might call throat-clearing addressed to the abbess herself: he praises Petronilla, alludes to Robert's special qualities and the sadness caused by his death, and then makes excuses for what is to come based on various authorial failings and distractions plus the skimpy notes Petronilla provided to him for his project. Having promised to do his best, Baudri begins the narrative, but not before several hundred additional words of encomium and more apologies for inadequacy. Finally, upon invocation of the Holy Spirit, Baudri begins the chronological recounting of Robert of Arbrissel's life and accomplishments. These twenty sections describe the various stages of Robert's life and divide into two nearly equal parts: activities before and after the foundation of Fontevraud. Sections 7 through 16 tell of Robert's birth, studies in Paris, return to Brittany as a reforming archpriest in the diocese of Rennes, additional study at Angers, life as a hermit, foundation of La Roë, commission to preach by Pope Urban II, and itinerant evangelism.

In section 16, Baudri narrates the original settlement of Robert's diverse followers at Fontevraud (far removed from Rennes, Angers, or La Roë) and describes their idyllic life under his guidance. After an excursus on his subject's ascetic behavior, preaching, and appeal to his listeners—some of whom not only changed their lives after hearing Robert but even chose to join him as disciples—Baudri discusses the formalization of Robert's quasi-utopian community, the construction of permanent buildings, and the group's female leadership: in short, its transformation into a monastery. Baudri then reports on Robert's continued evangelical ministry, his foundation of daughter houses on the model of Fontevraud, and miracles of healing, exorcism, and pacification. After a brief account of Robert's decline and death in the daughter house of Orsan, the last sentence of the *vita* returns Fontevraud's founder to his foundation, where he was buried.

Baudri's brevity and his choice of material may reflect compromise between authorial aspiration, genre, and the wishes of his patron, Abbess Petronilla. In its discussion of the holy man's special traits, this *vita* follows some of the conventions of hagiography. Baudri concentrates throughout on Robert's religious ardor and its effects on others around him, from his days as the agent of clerical reform in Brittany to his final preaching and teaching. However, Robert's miracles, although of types standard in saints' lives, are remarked rather than recounted. Indeed, the whole question of sanctity is very much at issue: only once, in the introductory address to Petronilla, does Baudri apply the adjective *sanctus* to his subject. And although Fontevraud looms large in the second half of the chronological account, the name of the house is mentioned only four times during its course, and Petronilla's name but once.

What are the themes in this *vita?* To the extent that it transcends a chronological account, it coheres largely by dint of the insistence on Robert's personal magnetism and effectiveness, his ability to draw crowds of listeners mixed in age, sex, and social status and to change their lives. (Some scholars have found in Robert, at least in his evangelical and charismatic dimension, a protector of women and the humble against the small elite of lay- and churchmen who dominated the society of his day.) Baudri is quite explicit about Robert's broad appeal, to the extent of finding him what St. Paul aimed to be: all things to all people. Evidently the lure was partic-

ularly strong for women, and Robert recognized female competence and authority when he made two women the leaders of
Fontevraud. But this charisma was deployed across a very restless
career: after a stay of unknown length in Paris, Robert spent four
years in the city of Rennes, another two in Angers, two more in
solitary spiritual pursuit and guiding his foundation at La Roë,
then perhaps a few more in the early stages of settlement at
Fontevraud. Most of Robert's last two decades were spent on the
road and took him (as we know from other documents in this
book) everywhere from Rouen, in Normandy not far from the English Channel, to Agen in southwestern France. After leaving his
post in Rennes in 1093, he held no title other than the honorific
"master," refused to be or be called "abbot," and ultimately left
first the canons of La Roë and subsequently the sisters and brothers of Fontevraud to guide themselves. Perhaps for this reason,
Baudri is careful to underline the orthodox aspects of Robert's career: his study in Paris, diocesan responsibilities, biblical evangelism, papal commission, and foundation of traditional religious institutions. What motivated Robert, what drove his restlessness?
Does his varied career reflect evolution toward an end or simply an
organic series of Christian vocations? Were Fontevraud and its
satellite houses the center of his life in his last years, or did preaching come first in his mind? Baudri's account raises all these questions, which apply to the remainder of the evidence about Robert,
too.

TEXT: PL 162: 1043–1058. Here, as with other PL text editions, I have
occasionally chosen alternate readings suggested by the notes and
silently corrected some typographical and editorial errors.

Baudri, by the grace of God bishop of Dol, although unworthy,
to Christ's handmaid Petronilla, venerable abbess of the monastery
of Fontevraud, and to all the nuns in that monastery under her
rule: greetings.

1. By no means without reason, but rather to instruct you as a
spouse of God,[1] do I call to mind a maxim like *Listen, my daughter,*

and see [Ps 44/45:11]. Indeed you have listened, and truly heard the voice of Him who proclaimed *Leave your country and your kindred* [Gn 12:1].[2] You left your estates, you fled your paternal hearth, you rejected the seductive lures of the flesh that enticed you, and you came to Fount Evrald [*Fons Evraldi,* that is, Fontevraud] where you found and drank from the copious fount, the fount of preaching, the fount of religion: Lord Robert, the extraordinary word-scatterer[3] of our time, a great and distinguished teacher, admirable in word and deed, a man to be exalted and imitated. Here at last you remained among the sisters. Once instructed in a holy way of life, you forgot your relatives and your father's house [Ps 44/45:11], and through Lord Robert's efforts under the guidance of the Holy Spirit you were promoted to abbess—even though you had formerly done service in the unquiet of the marriage-bed.[4] Not without cause do the needs and concerns of the Holy Church often overshadow human institutions. Therefore God raised you to this high seat and, with the assent of Pope Pascal, put you in charge of His people.[5] How that begging, orphaned crowd needed such a mother! With such a steward, I say, these women could be supported, inasmuch as they accepted poverty for God's sake. You do well if you exert yourself wholly in providing for them, if you offer yourself up as a beast of burden to the responsibility you have shouldered and consider yourself to be the least of all your sisters.

2. The aforementioned Robert has gone the way of our fathers and, as we believe, having shed his mortal form, he has received the cloak of immortality [1 Cor 15:53–54], crowned by God. Whether remembrance of him is more cause for weeping or rejoicing is difficult to decide: human nature makes us weep for the absence of our dearest friend, and yet since our Robert has flown away to intercede for us in our God's court, sure faith commands us to rejoice. Because we do not yet know which of the two is particularly fitting, for the moment let us exert ourselves in both tears and gladness, and carry on step by step until we are removed from this vale of tears. Therefore let our eyes weep and overflow because our

good and eloquent master, the friend of God, has departed from
us. Let our hearts rejoice because our Robert has gone before us
from the filthy exile of this world to the dwelling place destined
for us.

Most beloved Mother, you have instructed me in my
insignificance to describe Robert's way of life as long as he lived
here on earth, how far removed it was from the common run of
humanity—to the extent it can be committed to writing—so the
account might hereafter, somehow, be of use to human frailty.
Since we find the traces of the Fathers in writing, so much more
willingly do we imitate those on whom we rely as intercessors
when we pray.[6] Of course this work should aim at Vergilian or Ciceronian style.[7] Lady Petronilla, you have imposed a great burden
that weighs heavily on my feebleness, since the great storm of the
wave-tossed world and, especially, of Brittany, where I live surrounded by scorpions, troubles me. Twin and savage ferocity will
surround me.[8] Next, how will one whom no drop of the Sallustian
bucket ever moistened hew to the rhetorical style of writing?[9] I ask
you: by what rash daring will I, mouth agape and overwhelmed by
multifarious sins, name the holy and righteous Robert? Finally,
what shall I say? You gave me a few notes that contained next to
nothing about Lord Robert, except that he was of Brittany stock.

3. Nevertheless when I remember how I have heard that God offers his grace even to the unworthy and recall that I have read how
the highest Creator gave for a time the power of human speech to a
brute animal, the ass,[10] I do not doubt that He *who makes the mouths
of babes articulate* [Wis 10:21] will inspire in me that same eloquence—not according to my merits, but to those of the oft-mentioned Robert. He will, if He wants, pour forth through this lead
pipe crystal-clear water for the benefit of future generations. Holiest sisters, as partaker in your prayers (to which I commend myself
especially), I will try to say a little about our master for whom you
sigh continuously. But I fear that, wanderer as I am, I will fail along
the way. If I say anything well in the attempt, I beg you to reckon it
a gift of God; if otherwise, as I am very much afraid, attribute my

failure to decrepit old age or trembling hands, to indolence, or, finally, to my inveterately sinful way of life. Yet remember that all men except one have lived in slavery to sin.[11] Farewell.

4. Let us thank the Lord our God, who even now does not stop coming to us, like the morning sun *rising from on high* [Lk 1:78]. And no wonder, since the Truth foretold it, since Jesus himself promised it in these words: *Behold, I am with you always, to the end of the world* [Mt 28:20]. If God is with us, how can Emmanuel, maker and master of all things, be idle among us? How can there be day without light, or fire without heat, ice without cold, or sun without brightness? And since never and nowhere can God be idle, so He worked conspicuously in our presence and in our times when he gave the world the venerable Robert of Arbrissel as a mirror, a stifler of vices, a propagator and teacher of virtues, a solace and guide for all forsaken and wandering souls. This Robert, ray of the rising sun, unflinching bearer of light, mighty preacher, illuminated the western region of the globe, and brightened the shadows of ignorance with his powerful voice.

5. I, Baudri, archbishop of Dol,[12] although unworthy, acquiesce to the wishes of the nuns of Fontevraud. I have taken up the duty entrusted to me, to expound (although in unpolished style) a way of life admirable among mortals, so that the sweet odor of his example may linger into the future and his teaching aid instruction in communal Christian life.[13] Whatever the record of memorable deeds, the matter will be more than the sequence of text will show. Most of Robert's story, matters about which my ignorance weighs heavily against me, is better left to a more celebrated writer.[14] Furthermore, many years, old age turned toward forgetfulness, also hold me back and blunt my ability. Therefore, I undertake this work unsupported by literary expertise, since at least I trust in the Lord. May the Holy Spirit sustain my obedience,[15] and the holiness of Lord Robert favor me. Amen.

6. As I begin my reply concerning the venerable Robert, I call upon the Holy Spirit, the bearer of truth, without whose aid the loquacity of logicians is silent and the reasoning of philosophers

obtuse, to give whatever help is fitting to this undertaking. So that
we may consider more deeply the basis of Robert's history, we will
treat briefly the matters of his homeland, parentage, and the times
in which he grew up, to bring forward the evidence of truth in each
matter. We will not seem to err if we first discuss his origins.

7. The blessed Robert of whom we have resolved to speak was
son and heir of the Christian profession[16] and a scion of lower
Brittany, which province he adorned as a priest. He was born in the
territory of Rennes, a native inhabitant of the village of Arbrissel.[17] His father was named Damilioch, his mother Orguende.
From boyhood, Robert began to develop mature habits and did
not carry on in the wanton ways characteristic of youth. Rather he
embraced radiant chastity, insofar as he was able,[18] and inwardly
loved cleanliness. He seemed to chase through the world after
swift-moving literary studies, for which he had been readied since
infancy but had been unable to pursue.[19] Restlessly he traversed regions and provinces, and was not able to be other than single-
minded in the pursuit of learning. And since at that time France
was flourishing more richly in scholarly labors, he left his native
land and, like an exile and fugitive, went to France, and entered the
city called Paris.[20] There he found the teaching in literature pro-
portionate to his longing, all that he had determinedly sought, and
there he began to read incessantly. He exerted himself in this
quest, but did not on that account neglect to follow an acceptable
way of life. Among his fellow students he exhibited a kind of dignity, a measured austerity, and by various signs showed clearly what
his future was to be. At that time King Philip, son of King Henry,
ruled the lands of the Franks, and Gregory VII held the papacy in
Rome;[21] I give this information to indicate clearly in what era
Robert grew up and pursued his studies. He rendered to the scholars what was the scholars' but did not thereby apply himself any
less to the service of God.[22] Those who got to know him at that
time already foresaw his fate, since they observed something of
greatness in him.

8. Meanwhile the city of Rennes, bereft of its patron, had recourse to God in prayer and chose as bishop a certain Sylvester, whom both moral integrity and high birth rendered suitable. Noble by blood, he was nobler still in merit, and although not very learned, he eagerly embraced the company of learned men. Indeed his spiritual discipline was so strong that what flesh and blood had not inspired in him, divine teaching instilled splendidly. Therefore he brought together learned men from wherever he could find them, for that sort of person was quite rare in Brittany. In the course of his search, Sylvester heard about Robert, his austerity and zeal. Sylvester's informants said to him, "This Robert of whom we speak is your own countryman, from Rennes, and quite suitable to your purposes: he is exceedingly well versed in literary learning, vigorous in body, and studied in good conduct." Transport prepared, the venerable bishop headed to Paris. He sent for Robert and spoke to him thus. "You see, dearest brother," he said, "how your Holy Mother Church of Rennes wanders without direction—especially now, since it has fallen to me, a near-layman, to be at her helm. I beg you, be my spokesman in ecclesiastical affairs. I will hear you, and you will speak through me. There is no doubt that you will benefit the people of God, if in godly zeal you decide to serve us for a while."[23]

9. Robert acceded to the bishop's entreaties and henceforth solicitously took up ecclesiastical affairs and concerns. He kept God before his eyes in every undertaking, was lax in nothing, drove from himself desire for shameful profit and conducted himself lawfully in every instance. He supported his bishop faithfully in all matters, for Sylvester, although Robert's patron, did not scorn the patronage of his protégé. For four years Robert remained the bishop's archpriest. While restoring peace among those at odds, freeing the church from shameful servitude to lay people, and putting a stop to the sinful fornications of clergy and laity, he utterly abhorred simony, and manfully opposed all vices.[24]

10. After four years the bishop, stricken by grave illness, shed his

mortal form and, as we believe, departed for the heavens. Robert remained, alone, an orphan among orphans—alone, I say, because his fellow clerics resented his probity, and already their resentment had turned to hatred. He decided to yield in face of their ill will and, following the word of his Master, to flee from one city to another [Mt 10:23]. He did not want to be a stumbling block for anyone, which he knew full well to be a great and grave sin.[25] So he went to Angers, and settled into scholarly studies there. Nor on that account did he grow lukewarm in religious fervor, for he proceeded to read in divine philosophy.[26] He avoided idleness, devoting himself alternately to prayer and reading. Resolving firmly to master the lures of flesh, he wore an iron tunic next to his skin. He continued this practice for two years before going out into the desert, where he gave himself up wholly to contemplation.[27] During those two years in which he tamed the flesh with the iron tunic he wore fine cloth over it to hide himself from men's eyes and favor and reveal himself only in God's sight. For he despised fawning folly his whole life and spurned flattery as if it were poison. At some times he ate sparingly of meager meals, at others he spent the night awake in prayer.

11. The day came when Robert, renouncing the world, sped away to the wilderness he had so long desired, in the company of a certain priest. He stayed in the forest, rejecting the society of men to become the companion of beasts. Who could worthily recount how completely and with what savagery he raged against himself, how many and severe the tortures he inflicted on himself, with what grim horrors he weakened himself? For beyond the outwardly visible—like wearing a pig-hairshirt, shaving his beard without water, scarcely knowing but one blanket, refraining altogether from wine and from rich or fine food, abusing natural frailty by rarely getting half a night's sleep—there was also internal conflict, a kind of roar in his mind and a sobbing in the depths of his soul, which you could think cruel and impious and susceptible to no lasting remedy, and which, many murmured, was too much, impossible for

claylike brittleness [sc. of human flesh; see Jb 4:19–20]. He quarreled with God in incomparable wailing and pledged his whole self
as a sacrifice. Mild and gentle with everyone, Robert was an im-
placable enemy at war with himself alone.

12. To crowds of comers—for a great many people came to see
him—he was cheerful and pleasant, friendly and courteous, pru-
dent in doubtful matters, quick in replies. He gave off something
like the perfume of divine expressiveness, for few were his equal in
eloquence. So it happened that many, after hearing him, were
heartstruck and renounced their wicked ways. Some returned
home, improved by his preaching; others desired to linger with him
and asked to enter into his service and stay with him as permanent
companions. He would have fled these throngs of his own accord
and hidden himself away all alone had he not been afraid to incur
blame on that account. For he had read *Let him who hears say, 'Come'*
[Rv 22:17]. Therefore it was incumbent on him to mete out the talent granted him, which the Lord coming from the wedding demanded with interest.[28] He realized that he should gather many together, and give them something to eat, lest they grow weak along
the way, since certain of them had come a long distance [Mk
8:1–3]. Those gathered together were called "regulars," who tried to
live in the way of the early Church under a rule. And therefore this
multitude [lit. swarm], fleeing from the enticements of the world,
became a congregation of canons.[29] Robert presided over them,
teaching them in the honeyed way of a very wise bee.[30] They built
a common dwelling and lovingly embraced his authority in teaching.

13. It happened in those days that the Roman pontiff Urban II
had come to Gaul as urgent affairs required and turned to stop in
Angers.[31] He heard about Robert, for such great light ought not be
hidden under a bushel [Mt 5:15, Mk 4:21, Lk 11:33]. The pope ordered him to be summoned, for he eagerly desired a conversation
with Robert. Urban prepared to solemnly consecrate a church, to
which ceremony you might think the whole of the earth flocked.[32]

The pope ordered Robert to speak to this great gathering and he commanded him to use his accustomed discourse.[33]

14. Robert spoke brilliantly to the people, and his words pleased the Lord Pope immensely, for Urban understood that the Holy Spirit had opened up his mouth [Ps 50/51:17]. Next the pontiff ordered and enjoined on Robert the office of preaching; he insisted on the duty of obedience when Robert hesitated a little. The pope appointed Robert his second as God's word-scatterer[34] and urged him to pursue this mission wherever he went.

15. Henceforth, Robert began to apply himself diligently to his commission from the highest pontiff, traversing the territories of neighboring dioceses. He was honored by all, both because he was worthy of honor and because God's grace manifestly went along with him. His language was neither arid nor idle and a retinue praiseworthy in words and deeds entrusted itself to it. Robert practiced what he preached, lest he himself be condemned straightaway as worthless for having preached to others what he did not fulfill himself. Such a great crowd attached itself to him that the number of his canons might almost have been thought nothing at all. The number would exceed reckoning if only a tenth of the worshipers had joined the community of canons. Great-hearted Robert did not want to fail anyone if the will and rule of the canons permitted. Therefore he planned to leave the brothers, but considered also how he could do so without harming them.[35] In the presence of the bishop of Angers, in whose diocese the canons lived, it was decided that, both in accordance with the situation and the command of the Lord Pope,[36] and with the bishop's counsel and the permission of the canons, Robert departed, in order to be more free for his preaching vocation and able to serve wherever and whomsoever, unimpeded.

16. Robert, torn away from the canons with tears on all sides, began to traverse regions and provinces and, at first joined by a few followers, scattered the seed of God's word in highways and byways. In short order many people of both sexes joined him, be-

cause he did not dare turn away anyone whom God might have inspired. He himself *had no place to rest his head* [Mt 8:20, Lk 9:58] except that which necessity demanded. After he left the canons, he
did not want to settle down in any one place, so that he could go
forth, free, without staff or pouch [Lk 10:4]. But he saw that the
number of his followers was increasing. Lest anything be done ill-
advisedly, since women should remain with men, he resolved to
seek out a place where they could live and share communal life
without concern for scandal, if he could procure a deserted spot.[37]
There was a rough and neglected place, thick with thorn and
bramble, long called Fount Evrald [*Fons Evraldi,* that is, Fonte-
vraud]. It was removed from human habitation, about two miles
from the monastic cell of Candes, adjacent to the diocese of
Poitiers. Robert chose this little forest or thicket as the place where
God's new family and new army would live and work. He took it
as a gift from certain landowners, and led his mixed crowd of
Christian recruits there.[38]

17. For the time being Robert's flock built some huts to keep
them at least sheltered from the elements. They also built a little
oratory there, in which God was invoked and welcomed amidst the
camps.[39] The troops especially desired to speak with their God and
chose first of all to ready themselves for that conversation. Next
they proceeded to work, so that they were able to live by the labor
of their own hands, and never presume to be idle.[40] Nevertheless
Robert separated women from men, and sentenced to the cloister,
so to speak, those he set aside for prayer; the men he literally delivered over to labor.[41] He did so with wise discernment: he committed the gentler and weaker sex to psalm-singing and contemplation
and the stronger sex to the duties of the active life. Laypeople and
clerics went about together, except that the clergy sang psalms and
celebrated Mass, while the layfolk voluntarily submitted to labor.[42]
Certain times were appointed for collective silence. Robert's followers were ordered to speak kindly and not to swear oaths [Mt
5:34]; all were joined together in fraternal love. There was no bitter-

ness among them, no jealousy, no strife. They went about with
neck bowed and face down. Refraining from babbling, they were
strangers to idle chatter. This was the covenant to which they submitted, this the law under which they battled. They called their
leader only "Master," since he did not want to be called "Lord" or
"Abbot."[43]

18. For a long time Robert had no packhorse and tasted neither
wine nor seasoned food. He always went about barefoot and wore
very rough tunics and sackcloth until, at the urging of priests and
in recognition of a tiring body, he got on a beast of burden and
wore shoes. He indulged his worn body a little, not for pleasure,
but only to be strong enough for his work. He guarded against
longing fulfillment of fleshly desires [Rom 13:14]. He joined one fast to
the next and often spent whole nights in prayer; by day he wore
down his limbs with starvation, and made each practice worse
without any discomfort. He tore out all hypocrisy at the roots, was
cheerful and pleasant of face, natural and charming in reply, lavish
in alms. Chary with himself, he was very generous to his brothers
and sisters. In sermons he seemed to damn sinners, but those for-
saking sin he comforted with paternal affection. So it happened
that many sinners male and female[44] attached themselves to him
and obeyed him with their whole strength. For he sent no wanderer away, but in the end cherished in his breast any penitent he welcomed there. His speech could not but be effective because he was,
as I might say, *all things to all people* [1 Cor 10:33]: mild with the repentant, severe with the wicked, charming and approachable with the
sorrowful, a club against the irreverent, a staff for the old and wa-
vering, groaning in his heart, moist-eyed, serene in counsel. Really
I might call him a dwelling place of Jesus Christ, a temple and organ of the Holy Spirit, and a vicar and deputy of the Most
High.[45]

19. The crowd of those renouncing sins, steeped in Robert's
words, grew such that their number could hardly be counted. He
wanted them to be called by no other name than "Christ's poor."

Many men of every rank flocked to him, and many women gathered, poor and noble, widows and virgins, old and young, whores and those who spurned men.[46] No longer did the huts already built suffice to shelter an innumerable flock; Christ's recruits required roomier dwellings. Every means of support became available to him who fed the children of Israel in the wilderness with his fragrant plenty [Ex 16]. Robert supported with his own rations this his poor and begging family in the thickets, even when they did not yet plow, nor sow, nor reap. For the God of all inspired all the neighboring inhabitants to send Robert's flock a daily ration, to prepare a daily banquet for them. Nor could this have been done without God, who continued to inspire in local people the desire to send food. Whatever was given came through the workings of grace, and through the workings of grace God was praised when anything was lacking. In neither case did the community want to be ungrateful, for they joyfully gave thanks for the present and awaited the future, sure and hardy in their hope. They received abundance and bore want without complaint, but in either case God was praised. Robert, the mother bee, the very wise bee, went forth to look for food. When he talked with people, everyone not only sent nourishment to the family of God, but also freely gave donations of clothing to cover their nakedness and gifts for the construction of dwellings.[47] There was one common will, one unfailing abundance; the donors' wealth seemed to increase, for they suffered no want on account of their charity. Princes and common folk came to visit the new family of God, pale and withered under its rule of thrift. Nor did the hungry leave there before they heard an edifying word and tasted the bread of charity for the sake of the community.

20. Already, then, collective labor began to broaden and raise the walls of the oratory. Great wealth was donated, everything needed was offered, and cloister after cloister was prepared, for not even three or four sufficed for such companies of women. Men were separated from women and house after house was made ready

for them, at a distance, in secluded places. The wise master separated the women further, and then assigned them to cells and corners.[48] He arranged both men and women together in groups, since the number of both increased in honor.[49] In the major cloister he settled more than 300 women; to other places he committed 100, or 60, or other quantities, more here, fewer there.[50] Similarly he assigned men in separate companies.

21. Robert did not want to assist the workmen, nor could he have, since he had to preach to many peoples. Therefore he named one of the sisters, Hersende by name, as commander and directress for business and building. Disregarding her considerable nobility, Hersende joined the ranks of the women; indeed, she had converted to religious life earlier. She was a woman of great religious faith and great judgment in each measure. To Hersende Robert joined Petronilla, an expert property manager, whom Robert later chose as abbess (for Hersende had gone on to her reward). Because he knew these two women to be wise, hard-working, and very discreet, he put them in charge, as the saying goes, of the other sisters. Concerned with these matters up until then, Lord Robert was never afterwards distracted from preaching or prayer in any circumstances, but was wholly devoted to his mission as he moved about regions near and far.[51] He was received by kings, bishops, and princes, the clergy, and every sort of layperson.

22. Kings and nobles sent generous donations to the treasury of the very modest monastery of Fontevraud. Lords and almost everyone else gave what seemed needed. Some gave their estates, others made over allowances.[52] So it happened that in a short time the monastery had grown in houses and oratories, even in household goods. In turn, the inhabitants gave generous alms from what they had been sent; they took in the poor and did not reject the frail. Nor did they refuse unchaste women,[53] concubines, lepers, and the helpless. For lepers, Master Robert built little houses as well as nuns' cloisters and arranged that each group be cared for; as long as he lived, he often and most humbly visited such people himself.[54]

Robert attended Mass with total devotion, sobbing, and, to coin a phrase, he never knowingly tolerated anything impious. He was the sole lord, ridden with anxiety because he was considered the calm in the crowd.[55] Any discussion with him was a moral education, for whatever he said savored of God. Although there was need for many stonecutters and masons and other artisans, Robert appeared to put concern for those things behind him, since his soul was concerned with holy religion alone. Whose pen, do you think, will describe Robert exactly, he whose mind, whose understanding, whose soul always clung to God? The more I say about Robert the more dumbfounded I become. Since I discover what more still ought to be told about him, but I am in no way qualified for the telling, it is as if I had said nothing. Behold: overcome, I desist, and blushing, I am driven to confess that his abundance has rendered me inarticulate.

23. Look: we have discussed Robert's praiseworthy way of life for some time, and although we appear to have said something, it is actually almost nothing at all—we are eager to portray one who thrived in such intimacy with God, but we are unequal to the task. Through whom has God wrought more plentiful miracles in our time? Is it not perfectly evident that Robert was an imitator of the One who said, *The spirit of the Lord is upon me; He sent me to bring good news to the poor* [Lk 4:18]? Robert in truth brought the good news to the poor, called the poor, and gathered them together. For if any woman of the nobility made haste to him, the wise one sometimes resembled Nicodemus and Jesus, at others the centurion Cornelius and Peter.[56] He attracted all people with the wealth of God's grace and sent no one away, because *he wants everyone to be saved* [1 Tm 2:4]. Let anyone declare what he thinks, but I boldly say that Robert was abundant in miracles, he had power over demons, and he was glorious beyond worldly princes. Who in our age cured so many sick people, cleansed so many lepers, raised so many from the dead?[57] He who is of the earth and speaks of the earth [Jn 3:31] marvels at bodily miracles. But the spiritual person witnesses the weak, leprous, and dead being made well again whenever anyone

tends to and heals weak and leprous souls in need of cure. So finally let me ask, with the leave of all: through which of His pastors
has the Lord spoken and accomplished so much?

24. Our contemporaries, and also we bishops and abbots, clergy
and priests, have all entered into the labors of others [Jn 4:38] and
we have grown fat on the poverty of those who endured it before
us. Perhaps we are of little use and—fearful thought—possibly
these words are aimed at us in reproach: *Wickedness oozes out as from
their fat* [Ps 72/73:7]. This Robert, this man, I say, was wholly impoverished for Christ, exiled from his homeland and his family.
For Christ's sake he built homes for the poor in the solitude of
Fontevraud (without much in the way of resources of any kind),
lest he seem to fail the crowds that had pressed around him when
he preached.[58] He saw to it that oratories were built—he put down
the first foundation and the first stone and gathered more than
2,000, in fact nearly 3,000 servants and handmaids of God. He
founded great armies of Christians in cells and across regions and
provided for their material support.[59] To go so far in such a short
time would have been an extremely difficult task for mighty kings.
Now then—who would not testify that this beggar, this indigent,
this pauper, was rich? Rich indeed, he who was able to accomplish
such great and lasting deeds not for himself, but for God, and who
was able to feed so many hordes in the desert.[60] But to speak more
truthfully, Robert himself could not do all this. That it did happen makes it perfectly clear that God was the giver and master,
Robert the steward and agent. The one rained down copiously,[61]
the other faithfully distributed the drops. They seemed to have had
a certain friendly competition: which of them could do more, the
One providing, or the one dispensing? Truly God knew that
Robert was a faithful deputy when He brought together his family
and increased its fortune. So it is written: *Good and faithful servant,
whom the Lord has placed over his household* [Mt 24:45]. How could these
things have happened without God? I declare, and declare truly,
that those whose prayers were not out of harmony certainly had

their deeds in accord. And these are miracles, in case you do not know, beyond those the blessed Robert accomplished: to love God, to serve God, to respond so effectively to Lord Robert's wishes, and to supply through his hand everything that his followers needed.[62] Robert knew faith in the One whose will he sought not to offend. As long as Robert lived, God always exalted him, so that His family in Robert's hand might daily increase and continuously be granted largess to allow all things to be fulfilled.

25. Even as time passed, Robert never flagged in the promise he had made to God, and was ever more passionate in love of God, ever fresh, ever more devoted. As the years went by, the blessed man knew by certain signs that his end was approaching, for his limbs were becoming weak and his bodily strength failing. He decided to go visit and greet the brothers and sisters, and so he went. He strengthened all in the Lord and spoke to each one with kind words. He entrusted his death to his fellow disciples and exhorted them never to become lukewarm in their good practices.

26. Having had conversations with each sex, having received Holy Communion, in the face of likely death Robert spent himself in greetings and good works. As his illness increased—God was indeed summoning his pupil—in a place called Orsan, with a sobbing crowd by his side, Robert gave up the ghost and then, as we believe, ascended to the heights, to enjoy there eternal bliss as an abiding deacon of heaven, made the *heir of God and the joint heir of Christ*, as the Apostle puts it [Rom 8:17]. His wasted body, moistened by the abundant tears of the family of God, especially those of Christ's handmaids, was brought back to the monastery of Fontevraud, and buried in a fitting sepulcher in the reign of King Louis in France, and during the papacy of Pascal in Rome, Jesus Christ Our Lord reigning for all time.[63] Amen.

ANDREAS OF FONTEVRAUD, *SECOND LIFE OF ROBERT OF ARBRISSEL* (CA. 1120)

It is easy to imagine why Abbess Petronilla would have been dissatisfied with Baudri's account of the founder of Fontevraud. Baudri chastised his patron for not providing enough information, emphasized her married state, and said that Hersende would have been Robert's choice as abbess if she had lived. Robert's idiosyncratic, even erratic, career is on full view in Baudri's *vita*, which hints at even more peculiarities than it spells out. Fontevraud is not the centerpiece of Baudri's history. If Petronilla had hoped for an extended statement about the special character of Robert's mission as related to the establishment of Fontevraud and its federated monasteries, she was bound to be disappointed.

Probably it was Petronilla who commissioned a second account of Robert, this one focused on the last months of Robert's life and to a very significant extent on his guidance of Fontevraud and its priories. Its author insists on the plenitude of material that has necessitated selectivity to recount Robert's final months—an implicit answer to Baudri's grumbling about lack of information, since this second text is more than twice as long as the archbishop's sketch of Robert's career. The author of the new *vita* was Andreas, very likely Robert's chaplain, who accompanied him in his last days. This may be the same Andreas identified in other documents as the prior of Fontevraud, director of the brothers, who died between 1119 and 1122. Whoever he was, the author wrote before the spring of 1120, no more than four years after Robert's death. If he wrote anything else, it has not survived and there is no mention of it elsewhere. In fact, it is only by accident that all of Andreas's account is known to us. The last thirty-five sections, about forty percent of the *vita*, do not survive in the Latin Andreas wrote. Fortunately, around 1500 someone translated the entire manuscript into French, a text not uncovered until the 1980s by a French scholar, Jacques Dalarun. Although comparison of the French and Latin versions of the first forty-two chapters shows that the writer of ca. 1500 was not utterly faithful to the Latin text, its authenticity as a close paraphrase of Andreas's original is unquestionable.

One thing about Andreas is quite certain: he was a master storyteller and a careful literary artisan. His report of Robert's last months is dramatic and compelling. After a brief prologue, the narrative portion of the *vita* falls into five main episodes. In late summer of 1115, Robert consults with others about the possibility of naming an abbess for Fontevraud. Having decided to do so, and with the assurance of the male religious of their desire to continue to serve under the authority of women, he names Petronilla of Chemillé the first abbess of Fontevraud, providing her with a set of special rules for the organization of the abbey and its daughter houses (sections 3–10). The next part describes Robert's final tour, which takes him, over the course of two or three months, from Fontevraud to the priory of Hautes-Bruyères, just west of Paris, then finally to Orsan, a priory of Fontevraud in central France (sections 11–25). The third part (sections 26–54) relates in great detail Robert's words and actions in the days up to his death on February 25th, 1116. Here Andreas emphasizes Robert's prayerfulness and self-castigation and his desire that, since he is too ill to return to Fontevraud, his body be taken there after his death. Once Robert has died, a struggle ensues between those, led by Abbess Petronilla, who want to take the body back to Fontevraud for burial and a group of local churchmen and laypeople, led by Robert's patron Archbishop Leger of Bourges, unwilling to be deprived of this precious relic. Petronilla ultimately triumphs (sections 54–63). Andreas then narrates the journey back to Fontevraud, preparations for Robert's burial, and the ceremonies surrounding it (sections 64–68). A concluding section eulogizes Robert and illustrates his character and mission with a few anecdotes from his days of traveling (sections 68–75).

The structure of Andreas's text is notable for its elegance and symmetry. The chronicle that makes up almost the entire *vita* (sections 3–68) begins at Fontevraud, where Robert considers the institutional future of his foundation, and ends there with his burial. In the very middle of the narrative, Robert is shown asking various parties to assure his final return. The individual parts are carefully arranged, too: the brothers' pledge of loyalty (section 3) is a prelude to the election of Petronilla as abbess (sections 4–9), to which Robert's issue of written rules are the coda (sections 9–10). The conflict between the parties of abbess and archbishop over the fate of Robert's body reaches its dramatic peak in the very middle of the quarrel, when some of the archbishop's lay followers decide to withdraw from the contest and Petronilla organizes a procession of penance and protest by the nuns of Orsan. Not content with assembling details, Andreas carefully crafts his account so that each episode has its own rhythm. The dramatic character of the narrative is heightened by the extensive use of direct and indirect quotation. Of the fifty-two chapters of narrative up to Robert's death, Robert's speech is reported in forty-one, and he is quoted, sometimes at length, in over half of those. Robert's final days, and the subsequent contest over his body, are told almost entirely as a series of conversations. It is no accident that Andreas's final thought is about the continued efficacy of Robert's speech, since he has emphasized the power of words and the preaching of the Word throughout.

The most important secondary figure is Petronilla. Her election as abbess is the initial focus; she also joins Robert for portions of his travels, comes quickly when summoned to his deathbed, converses with him in his last hours, and afterwards manages to effect the return of his body to Fontevraud—even after it has been forcibly taken from her control. The portrait that emerges is of a vigorous and powerfully persuasive leader on whose loyalty and mastery Robert relied and in whom he placed his trust for the future of Fontevraud.

This *vita*, then, features Robert as the founder and guide of Fontevraud. But it also shows him as a peacemaker, a visitor of prisoners, a preacher and spiritual advisor, and a penitent Christian who bewails his own inadequacies—as far back as childhood gluttony!—while seeking prayers and forgiveness for his soul in the face of death. The dispute over where Robert is to be buried echoes a tension felt elsewhere in Andreas's account: between Fontevraud and the road, between Robert's monastic foundations and his urge, even compulsion, to preach, even on his deathbed. Andreas emphasizes the diversity of Robert's audience, who range in these last months from a count and an archbishop to highway bandits. Despite the focus on Christian institutions and on religious women and men, Robert remains a wanderer whose journeying stops only when he is too ill to go on.

In the end, Robert goes back to Fontevraud, although not quite as he had wished: he is buried not in the cemetery but in the abbey church. This deviation from Robert's last wishes must have had Petronilla's approval if, in fact, it was not her idea. Perhaps Petronilla feared that if left in a cemetery, Robert's body would lie under threat of another forced removal from the nuns' custody. But by burying the body in the abbey church, she assured that his cult would be private rather than public. Andreas's account, then, confirms Petronilla's authority as superior but may also contain an implicit criticism of her choice of mausoleum. Petronilla says that Robert, mortally ill, will be able to do nothing more for the nuns. Does Andreas fear that the memory of Robert is no match for his unique ability to keep the community of Fontevraud intent on its mission? In any case, he provides a vivid portrait of Robert and his relations with the variety of people he knew and encountered at the end of his life.

TEXTS: PL 162: 1057–1078 (sections 1–42) and Jacques Dalarun, *L'impossible sainteté: la vie retrouvée de Robert d'Arbrissel (v. 1045–1116), fondateur de Fontevraud* (Paris, 1985), 284–299 (sections 42–75)

1. Although the life of Master Robert was described by Baudri, the venerable bishop of Dol, in brilliant style, and Robert's noteworthy way of life and his moral integrity were recounted succinctly, I would like to recall briefly for posterity how Robert conducted himself at the end of his life and how he departed this world. However, I advise the reader of the present work that I will not mention in this treatise everything worth telling. Rather I shall record briefly what ought to be said. For if I wanted to recite one by one all the things the Lord deigned to accomplish through Robert in the last year of his life, I confess that, weighed down by such a mass of material, I would, against my will, be overwhelmed.[1] But since I have next to no literary art that would allow my modest intelligence to search out these matters, may the grace of the Holy Spirit assist me through the interceding merits of him about whom I am now to speak.

2. First, something should be said about why he was called Robert, for he did not get such a name without divine providence. He was named Robert, as in "strengthened," or "certain in strength."[2] In truth he was strong, because the Holy Spirit surely fortified him to do good always. And he was certain in the strength of his faith, persevering in holy religion right to the end of his life. A certain musical monk fittingly chanted about him:

"If you go looking, none like him will be in reach;
What sort and how great he was only witness of his success can teach."[3]

3. And so this Robert, for many years a tireless preacher, had dispersed the Word of God not only to neighbors but even to foreign peoples when bodily infirmity increased along with other, older ailments and he suddenly began to lose vigor.[4] Finally, de-

tained by illness at Fontevraud, lying in bed, he ordered all the brothers living there to be called to his side. After all had gathered quickly, he said, "Behold, my dearest sons, whom I begot in the Gospel [1 Cor 4:15], I am stricken with bodily affliction and am entering the way of all flesh. Therefore, consider among yourselves, while I am still alive, whether you wish to remain firm in your purpose, that is, to obey the command of Christ's handmaids for the salvation of your souls. You know that in every one of the houses that, with God's help, I have established elsewhere, I have placed you men under women's dominion and rule. But if you do not wish to remain with them as you began, I grant you freedom to choose another religious rule in consultation with me."[5] Having heard him, nearly all said with one voice, "God forbid, dearest father, that we ever abandon the sisters since, as you yourself attest, we can in no way do better anywhere else. God forbid," they said, "that we abandon your counsel. Rather, we all unanimously and freely promise before God and His saints stability and perseverance in the Church of Fontevraud."[6]

4. The congregation of our brothers and sisters having so agreed, Robert wanted to provide for the well-being of his posterity, instructed, as I believe, by divine inspiration. For after a few days passed during which he burned constantly with fever, he sent word by messengers to a number of bishops and abbots, commanding their presence so he could ask their advice. And since the Church of Poitiers was at that time bereft of its own patron and suffered under the dominion of Count William, he ordered some of its high officials be summoned to give counsel.[7] After not a small assembly of religious people and nobles had been gathered, he revealed his reasons for having had such a great multitude convene. "I sense, brothers, that my end is near, and therefore I have sent for you so that with your advice I might be able to provide beneficially for the future of our church with the election of an abbess." With one accord they answered him reverently: "Your plan concerning this matter, dearest Father, ought to be put into action,

especially since we are quite certain that your wisdom is equal to that of any mortal of our age. God gave you to the world as a counselor of souls, and with His help, it is very easy for you to offer counsel for the future life of your people."

5. Then he said to them, "You know, my dearest ones, that whatever I have created in this world I did for the sake of our nuns, and I gave them total control over my resources. And what is more, I submitted myself and my disciples to their service for the salvation of our souls. Therefore I have decided, with your advice, to appoint an abbess as the head of this community while I am still alive lest by some chance—God forbid—after my death someone presume to oppose this my decree. Therefore according to the dictates of the Wise One, I want to do everything with counsel, so I regret nothing after it is done [Sir 32:24]. For he who does his own works without the advice of elders shows himself unwise. I ask you one thing: is it permitted me to name a lay convert[8] as abbess, so that, after the fact, your valid authority will restrain any detractors? I know, I know: the dignity of this office calls for a virgin, for indeed it is written that whosoever watches over virgins should be a virgin.[9] But how will any claustral virgin, who knows nothing except how to chant psalms, be able to manage our external affairs suitably? What earthly matters has she effectively 'sung,' one who has always been accustomed to spiritual labor? How, I say, will she who knows nothing but the joys of contemplation shoulder the burden of the active life? With what skill will a tongue accustomed from childhood to speak with the Lord in prayer, singing, or reading reply concerning external affairs? Moreover it is very difficult to force one who rejoices in her washed feet to put back on the dress of temporalities.[10] I have read that the wise woman built her own house, but the foolish one tore it down [Prv 14:1]. Therefore, I do not want to entrust this office to any claustral virgin if in so doing I knowingly give a charge to one who does not know how to manage, lest I appear (let it never be so!) to destroy what I built, indeed what I built with God's aid. Therefore let a covering be cho-

sen that will protect the Lord's tabernacle,[11] and manfully weather the storms of external affairs, so that the scarlet glows inside with perfect color.[12] Let Mary attend ceaselessly to celestial concerns, but let us choose Martha, who knows how to minister wisely to external affairs [Lk 10: 38–42]."[13]

6. On hearing this, the elders present gave their assent and affirmed that everything Robert had said was true. And in order that Master Robert's decree would be held permanent and inviolable, there was among those present a certain archpriest of Angers, a man of honorable life, who affirmed that once when he was in Rome he heard the Lord Pope Urban (the same one who charged our Robert with the duty to preach)[14] allow a certain matron, who had had four husbands, to be made abbess according to the circumstances and need of a church. Clearly the man of venerable life knew that divine piety, everywhere maintaining moderation, does not punish that to which the necessity of human frailty, *salva fide*, constrains us. Having learned this story, the assembled company rejoiced and all said together that this wise Robert wanted to act wisely. Then, the holy conference at an end, the participants upheld the counsel of the astute Robert in their praise, and on two accounts they returned home from him with joy.

7. When September, in which the aforesaid assembly had taken place, had passed and the end of October was approaching, on the fifth kalends of November[15] our father concluded the business he had asked about, not without the counsel of religious men. He therefore chose for the position of such high honor Petronilla of Chemillé, who, her paternal wealth renounced, had been Robert's follower nearly from the beginning of her conversion to religious life and was of sounder counsel than many wise people. He said, "Indeed it seems fitting to me that one who bore along with me the labor of wandering and poverty should also bear any burden of support and prosperity.[16] Although she is once-married,[17] it seems to me that by virtue of necessity nobody is more suited to this prelacy. She knows our estates better than anyone and, as the

Apostle says, *how to be rich and to suffer poverty* [Phlm 4:12]. She knows both how to give an opportune response to the wise and how to condescend fitly to the simple."

8. After what the outstanding master had done was heard abroad, not only our brothers but also laymen praised a choice of this sort. Finally it was made known to Petronilla herself. How she wanted to avoid the election, and the ways she tried to decline it, is a long story. For she quite reasonably feared (because it was awesome) the immeasurable burden of taking up a place of such honor. On one hand, as a wise woman she feared her own weakness; on the other, she considered the immeasurable magnitude of the prelacy. What else to say? Although resisting greatly, at God's command and convinced by the prayers of her flock—or, more to the point, constrained by obedience to Master Robert—she agreed in the end. There are many things I could tell about her way of life that are worth telling. But because I confess that I am her son, however unworthy, I will be silent for the present, lest, God forbid, I be judged to anoint her head with the oil of flattery. So: the election of our very dear mother carried out with the common consent of religious men in this fashion, each one went home.[18]

9. Not long afterwards, when the oft-mentioned Robert, with God's favor, had begun to recover somewhat from his illness, he desired to confirm the election I have just described by the authority of the venerable legate Gerard of Angoulême. Gerard not only granted confirmation of the deeds of the wise Robert in his own capacity but also, what is more, sent messengers and procured a written privilege from the Roman pope Pascal concerning Robert's choice.[19] This is why our Robert made a general precept for the abbess he had chosen: never would any claustral nun be made abbess at Fontevraud. The holy man knew well that many monasteries were destroyed through the negligence and inexperience of abbesses raised in the cloister. And so that this precept be kept inviolate by posterity, it was committed to writing, among Robert's

other commands, which were written down at Fontevraud and are observed there to this day.[20]

10. The renowned Robert, the light of hermits, gave certain commands to his godly flock so that men and women united in spirit would guard the holiness of their religious life in speech, action, food, and clothing. For that man, worthy to be praised by every mouth, knew that *religion is vain* [Jas 1:26] if always accompanied by immoderate speech. He also knew that anyone boasts in vain that he has faith unless he joins that faith to good works. As the apostle James says, *Faith without works is dead* [Jas 2:20]. This kind man had also read that *It is good not to eat meat* [Rom 14:21]. Therefore he wanted himself and his family to abstain from such food for the love of God. He also knew how a cheap tunic shows contempt for the world and for that reason wanted himself and those subject to him to be dressed in common clothing. He said to us that such vestments as might ward off the cold of human frailty should suffice for all the community, but not those that exist to adorn a mortal body—which is doubtless secular and worthy of censure. This rule concerning clothing was established by him for our order, so that in accordance with the authority of St. Benedict, neither brothers nor sisters should be upbraided for the native color, coarseness, or size of their clothing.[21] But if anyone wants to know these commands in full, let him humbly ask at Fontevraud, where they were written down as much for the love of such a man as for his great gift.

11. This Robert of whom we are speaking had built a number of houses in different regions with God's help. In them he enclosed companies of nuns tested in holy religion at Fontevraud, in numbers according to the suitability of the place, and he appointed some of our brothers to serve them.[22] This, moreover, was his unswerving custom: wherever he had monasteries built for his nuns, he constructed them in honor of Holy Mary, ever virgin. And because St. John the Evangelist, at Christ's command, unfailingly served that same Virgin Mother as a devoted minister as long

as she lived bodily in this world, wise Robert decreed that the
brothers' churches should be dedicated to John. I think this must
have been done with divine inspiration so that the brothers would
rejoice to have as patron of their church the one they regard as an
example of service owed to the brides of Christ. I do not say so
because I want to compare our service to John's pleasurable duty,
believing as I do without a doubt that the most excellent Virgin,
seated next to her Son in heaven, is alone and without equal.

12. Those dwellings, in which this remarkable man enclosed the
Lord's sheep in consultation with local prelates, he often visited
like a good shepherd, so that if ever any incitement to wickedness
sprouted there at the Devil's goading, he could rip it out by the
roots according to his ability. It happened that with the permission
of Louis, king of the Franks, Robert was granted a certain deserted place in Gaul, commonly called then and now Hautes-
Bruyères.[23] Indeed he declined to have the convents of his holy
religion among castles or villages, knowing full well that these settlements were harmful to the purpose of monastic life. Once the
place was founded, during the course of the few years we are discussing, he sent along before him—through our abbess Petronilla
whom he had elected—some of our sisters for whom the place
had been specially built. Then the man of venerable life followed
them eagerly and without delay.

13. Robert and his party met for the purpose of respite one day
in the diocese of Chartres, in the village of Bonneval, where there
was a house of monks. At this time Ivo was bishop of Chartres,
and he had so quarreled over certain matters with Bernier, the abbot of Bonneval, that the differences between them were nearly un-
reconcilable.[24] Many religious people had tried numerous times to
bring about a settlement, but they did not manage to make peace
between the two. The pious master could not help but hear of such
a great conflict; he grieved for those at odds and began to mull
over how he could make peace between them. He sent his nuns on
ahead of him to the appointed place under the care of Angarde,

who was at that time the prioress of Fontevraud; then joining up with Abbot Bernard and Abbess Petronilla, he hurried to Chartres, hastening to reconcile the aforementioned dispute.[25] The peacemaker lamented that leaders of the Church were faithlessly in thrall to the impertinence of despicable dissension. To speak truthfully, after the wise orator came to Chartres, called forth by charity, he labored mightily. Not only did he utterly exterminate the devilish dispute, but also restored the two men to their former friendship—which many to this day find incredible.[26]

14. Peace restored between the leaders of the Holy Church, as Christmas was approaching, the aforementioned mediator of conflict arrived at Hautes-Bruyères, to which we referred a little earlier. Celebrating the Nativity of the Lord with the beloved daughters he had sent to that same place not long before with Angarde, Robert was unremitting in fasting, outstanding in prayer, insatiable in reading, wakeful in vigils, overflowing with tears, admirable in teaching. How many were the ways he sacrificed himself to God on the altar of his heart, or what harvest he gathered for God among his household and the crowds that flocked to him still remains, I suspect, unknown to mortals.

15. The beautiful feast of Christmas was celebrated with the greatest reverence at Hautes-Bruyères. Having provided for the spiritual and material well-being of the Lord's flock in that place, Robert, summoned to Chartres, went there again. The bishop of Chartres whom we mentioned above had died and another, unanimously elected by the clergy, had been enthroned in his place.[27] But there was such trouble between the clergy and the count of the city that some of the canons, having lost their property, feared that they would be torn limb from limb at the count's command.[28] For this reason a number of powerful people assembled at Chartres, even Abbot Bernard, worthy of the remembrance of all good people, whose praises are still sung today in all the churches of Gaul. But it was totally useless. They could not calm the disturbance, which in fact grew worse daily at the instigation of the Enemy of

all good people. For the ruler of the city had already ransacked the canons' dwellings, and shut them up in their cloister. Furthermore—it is wicked to speak of—he had driven away from the city the outstanding man, Geoffrey by name, whom the clergy had lawfully set in the place of the departed Ivo on the episcopal throne.

16. Why do I delay? By now the only hope for the canons, other than God, lay in our Robert. So it happened that through representatives they had asked for his help with every entreaty. Evidently the canons knew that God had given such great grace to the man of whom we are speaking that what was nearly impossible for others He for whom all things are possible [Mt 19:26, Mk 10:22, Lk 18:22] would deem worthy to effect through Robert. Although gravely ill, when asked if he would come to Chartres, Robert replied that all things were possible for him unto death. After his arrival, the outcome of the matter showed clearly how truly this was a servant of God, even if our tongue should keep silent. For the Lord had conferred such grace on Robert that not only did religious people hold him in awe but even kings and princes would most freely yield to his command. Indeed it was fitting that all creation love him whose good works left no doubt that he was loved by the Creator. Robert spoke to each party according to the wisdom God had granted him and by God's grace he utterly extirpated the whole devilish intrigue. At Robert's behest, the count of the city returned everything he had taken from the clergy, agreed to the election of Geoffrey, who had been chosen for episcopal rule by canonical procedure, and allowed him to return to the city. And—what is really delightful to say—Robert united them all together canonically in their bonds of former amity. I believe that the Lord wanted to snuff out this deathly homicide through his beloved Robert so that those who did not know might learn how much merit our Robert had with Him. It is not within my powers to sketch the quality and quantity of blessings the Lord saw fit to grant this oft-mentioned city through his servant in those times. Nevertheless, it is pleasing to report that the simoniacal heresy[29]

that had for a very long time defiled the canons' church at Chartres
was extinguished in perpetual condemnation through our Robert,
with the agreement of Bishop Geoffrey (whose life still smells so
sweetly in our time) and the cooperation of the canons, from the
greatest to the least in their community. And they swore a vow by
oath that this execrable plague would be completely and perpetual-
ly shunned in their church.

17. After the people of Chartres were pacified, the faithful steward of the Lord's Word left the city, never to return. Joining together with the venerable abbot Bernard of Tiron, whose company
had always been most pleasing to him, the two went to the castle
which is commonly called Blois. In that same castle the faithful
Christian count William of Nevers was held captive. The prisoner
himself was there to keep peace in the territories of King Louis of
France against the count of Chartres.[30] This William was held dear
by both men for the tested merit of his life. How great and honorable was the worthiness of this prince is clear from the fact that
these two pillars of the church came to visit him. He is said to have
been so heartened as to remark, "Who would not rejoice to be
long imprisoned in order that he could be visited by such men?" I
say these things in order to show that our Robert was never sloth-
ful, now visiting prisoners according to evangelical precept [Mt
25:43–44], now reconciling feuders to peace. After they had visited
with the count dear to them both, and heartened him even more
than his prison punishment required, these two visitors, never to
see each other again in this life, separated inseparably (as I might
say). They were inseparably separated because those whom love
joins distance does not divide. The bond of love is utterly indissol-
uble, since, as the Blessed Augustine says, "Love that can be divided was never true."[31] Oh if only they could have known that they
would never see each other again in mortal flesh! Indeed I believe
that scarcely ever or never would they have parted from one another in life if they had known that Robert's death was so close at
hand.

18. So Abbot Bernard then turned back home. But our pastor directed his path to the province of Berry, distributing lavishly the talent entrusted him.[32] The provident man knew full well that the more one person might edify by his example, so much more will he receive the Lord's reward on Judgment Day. For just as a fertile beehive disperses its swarms everywhere, so was our most pious father dispersing his honeyed troop of nuns from Fontevraud to other places. From this mystic hive of venerable bees, Robert had once upon a time apportioned a number of our sisters in Berry. In a place known as Orsan he had settled them in a wooden cloister he had first prepared for them, and now, doubtless out of love for them, he made ready to visit there while preaching in those same regions.[33]

19. But if we tell about just one thing that happened to him on the journey, we will show posterity clearly the extent of Robert's patience and holiness. A certain one of our brothers named Peter, illustrious in priestly office, faithful in word and life, who was with Robert at that time, recounted it to us thus. When they had begun the journey, one day they fell among thieves. Filled up with an evil spirit as is their wont, the brigands not only snatched his companions' animals but even (what is worse) they seized by the reins of the bridle the beast on which that gentlest of men sat and, afflicting him with insults, knocked him to the ground. But Robert, since he was truly kind, began to rebuke them piously in his dove-like voice and was exhorting them with gentle words to stop their thieving ways. I firmly believe that the merciful man was more grieved at the prospect of their perdition than at the trouble they caused him and his companions.

20. His comrade Peter, from whom I learned this, bore ill what had been done to his master and spoke in these terms to the robbers: "Tell me, wretches, where are you fleeing, you who have not feared to upset a man of such qualities? Think, I beseech you, think how much reverence ought be shown to holy men, that in this one way, at least, your senselessness may cease to rage [Sir 28:6]. For as Holy Scripture says, holy men are temples of God: *For*

God's temple is holy, and it is you, the Apostle says [1 Cor 3:17]. Therefore when a saint is roused to anger, it is naturally the case that
God, the dweller in the same temple, is provoked to vengeance. So
let your fury cease and let fruitful penitence wipe out the evil you
have done against God's holy one. Don't you know that this man,
whom you just now wrongly knocked off his horse, is Robert of
Arbrissel, whose sweet fragrance goes forth to the whole world?"
Hearing Robert's name, the crowd of bandits was at once utterly
petrified with fear. They fell at the holy man's feet, begging and
pleading for his pardon. Rejoicing at their contrition and petition,
Robert pardoned with equanimity whatever harm they had done
him, raised them up from his feet, and kindly kissed them. He not
only gave them the forgiveness they had asked, but also—which
they did not merit because of their sin—shared his favor with
them.

21. Oh ineffable man,[34] abounding with admirable faith, whom
neither prosperity gained with God's help beguiled, nor adversity
overwhelmed! Since, as it is written, *A man's learning may be known by
his patience* [Prv 19:11], it is perfectly evident how very patient and
outstanding in learning this Robert was, since he went so far as to
reward his enemies in the way we have just mentioned. Let us consider, if we can, with what ardent love this man of happy memory
cherished his friends, he who of his own accord, following the
Lord's teaching, rewarded his enemies with great favor [Lk 6:27].
Since Scripture says *Nothing that happens to him will sadden the righteous
man* [Prv 12:21] it is patently obvious that this man was the very
height of righteousness, who neither when provoked by enemies
nor for the sake of friends deviated from the right path.[35] It is perfectly fitting, brothers, for me to say that Robert was in this deed
like holy Samuel, who, wanting to retaliate against his enemies,
promised that he would pray for them [1 Sm 12:23]. Robert was in
accord with the one who said *I was peaceful with those who hated peace* [Ps
119/120:7]. What shall we wretches of Robert's congregation say
before God, we who do not even love our friends as we ought?[36]

22. After the lover of peace had peacefully parted from the ene-

mies of peace, he reached Orsan, where he was headed. The dissemination of faith went along with him.[37] He stayed at Orsan about two weeks with his beloved sons and daughters, unceasingly busy in reading, prayer, preaching, and other practices of virtue. There he awaited Abbess Petronilla, who was supposed to come to him from Fontevraud. When she had arrived, it pleased Robert to go out to preach since certain people, starved for the words of his preaching, had asked him to deign to share with them the favor of a holy sermon. Acquiescing to their pious pleas and desiring, with God's help, to satisfy their desirable hunger, he took to the road with Petronilla and some other companions. One day they arrived at the monastery of Déols in search of hospitality. The monks of that house happily received him, respectfully offered him the rights of hospitality, and very humbly asked him to deem it worthy to refresh their souls with the food of holy preaching.[38]

23. Moved by their entreaties, the Lord's bountiful word-scatterer[39] entered the monks' chapter house the next day with some of his companions, speaking at length in what was to be his last public sermon. Even those blessed to attend confess they cannot express how sweetly, how piously, how mercifully, how devoutly, how wisely, how charitably, how simply, how outstandingly—denouncing his hearers, beseeching, rebuking [2 Tm 4:2][40]—Robert told them to turn from sin and do good [1 Pt 3:11]. No wonder he accomplished his sermon so brilliantly, since through Robert God had offered the world so many great sermons, nearly incomparable according to those lucky enough to hear them. For the Lord had given him such a gift for holy preaching that whenever he addressed a crowd, each person there understood what was appropriate to himself. Nor was his preaching without effect: it so struck the hearts of his audience that it was quite clear who was there when Robert spoke. Certainly the Holy Spirit was present, without whose aid the speech of a learned man labors in vain outside himself, concerning which it is written *It is not you who speak, but the spirit of your Father* [Mt 10:20]. After he finished his sermon, he made full

peace with the monks of that place, who had a dispute with Fontevraud, and he even reconciled them and a certain local prince named Alard.[41]

24. These matters concluded, Robert told Petronilla and Angarde, the stewards of Fontevraud who were with him, to go visit their brothers and sisters. Together with his chaplain Andreas[42] he moved along to the people who so eagerly desired his preaching (as we said above) and who in their yearning had made many pleas. The day he left the monastery of Déols was a Friday. Along the way he began to get down from his packhorse more often than before and to show his companions that he was very ill. When they said, "Dearest father, turn back, we beg of you, turn back, before you are even more burdened by illness," he replied, "No, my sons, do not say such things to me, but let us proceed to the town called Graçay.[43] I promised people I would come. When they hear that I was on the way to them, let them at least believe that I turned back of necessity—if I am not able to complete the journey." Coming to Graçay, they were given hospitality there.

25. The next day, Saturday, our master was so ill that he could no longer ride at all. When he knew this, he said to his companions, "Make a wooden litter for me, my dearest brothers, and carry me back to Orsan, because I know I am going to die from this illness." When his host learned of the plan, he said, "Please, Master, do not do as you say, but instead rest here until you see if you are able to recover from this illness." But Robert said privately, as it were, to his companions, "Whatever others say, pay no mind, but do what I have told you, and do it quickly." It was very clear that he sensed his death was imminent, but lest his people be troubled with caring for his body, he wanted to return to Orsan while he was still alive. The wooden litter was prepared as he had asked and they carried him to the castle called Issoudun and were received there.[44] The host who welcomed him began to ask the party to allow the sick man to stay with him. When this reached Master Robert's ears, he called together his companions and said to them,

"My sons, do not accept the counsel of our host, but do just as I have already said to you: take me back to Orsan." Because, as we said above, he had sent Petronilla and Angarde to other places to visit the Lord's sheepfold [Jn 10:16], now sensing his end was near, he sent messengers after the two, telling them to come quickly to Orsan to see him.

26. Leaving Issoudun in the morning, they carried the very holy invalid to Orsan, as he had ordered. At that time a certain noble nun named Agnes was the prioress at Orsan. She was held in great affection in that place because on Robert's advice she had left behind the deceitful riches of the world, which had enticed her greatly, and instead chose poverty for Christ's sake.[45] It is not easy to express the magnitude of her grief when she heard of the Master's grave illness. Who indeed could tell what great sadness the brothers and sisters of that place felt when they had heard of the seriousness of our teacher's condition? They were sorely afraid of being deprived of such a remarkable pastor. On the Sunday evening when a very sick Robert had been carried into Orsan, he began to repeat piously the name of Fontevraud, saying, "Oh Fontevraud, Fontevraud, how I wanted to lie in you!" His faithful companion Andreas said to him, "Glorious Master, what are you saying? If you think this is the end, at all events tell us what you want: command us to take your body to Fontevraud after your death." Robert replied, "And why should my corpse be carried away from here? It would be taken away from you"—to use his exact words—"along the byways."[46]

27. The next day, Monday, he asked to be given the viaticum of the body and blood of Our Lord Jesus Christ. He saw that he still had a little longer to go, and therefore he asked with humblest devotion to be given this most healthful viaticum, without which any traveler might go entirely astray.[47] When the body of the Lord was brought to him, with inner groans and deep sighs he began to beg for gracious mercy from Him, to call himself a useless servant, and to reproach himself for all his deeds. This wise reader knew the

truth of what God had proclaimed: *When you have done all things that you were commanded, say: We are useless servants* [Lk 17:10]. Robert imitated that righteous man, who, even though he was perfect, said that he feared all his own works [Jb 9:28]. Indeed he had a twin lamentation: first he was deeply sorry that he had sometimes neglected the Lord's precepts, then he grieved that he had not observed all His commands. To sum it up in Robert's words: wailing, he lamented that he had been a useless servant in all things. After he reproached himself innumerable times and received a penance, presuming not at all on his own merits but praying continually for mercy, he received the body of the Lord. Let them hear this, who dare to receive the Lord's body carelessly, to their perdition: either they should efface their sins through holy penance, while it is possible, or, if they do not want to, then they should not dare to receive unworthily such a wonderful sacrament. The Apostle plainly cries out that *He who eats and drinks unworthily and without discrimination eats and drinks judgment on himself* [1 Cor 11:29]. If such an extraordinary man received the sacrosanct body of the Lord so timidly, much more should we sinners approach it trembling and weeping; even if we accomplish much, we dare not equate our end to his reward.[48]

28. Monday passed. Because the good man had no doubt that his death was close at hand, as a most Christian individual he wanted to take unto himself all the sacraments of the Holy Church. So on Tuesday he fervently asked that he might be anointed with blessed oil, doubtless believing the words of the Apostle James to the effect that through the operation of this mystery the sins of man are forgiven [Jas 5:14]. Anointed with the saving ointment, again he fortified himself with the Lord's body, not without inner sorrow. Not only on these two days did he fortify himself with Christ's Eucharist, but on all the days he lay ill. But who could describe how or in what ways he strove always to accuse himself before the body of the Lord? Those blessed to be there confess that if he had ever rebuked himself more before the Lord's body,

they knew nothing of it. Nobody, no thief, no bandit ever reproached himself thus, for as it is written: *The righteous man is his own
first accuser* [Prv 18:17]. It is patently clear that this man was righteous, who, although he had led an extraordinary life, nevertheless
accused himself so many times.

29. At that time Leger, a man flourishing in life and years, held
the archepiscopal seat at Bourges. Unless I am mistaken, inseparable love joined him fast with Master Robert; such mutual love
yoked them, as I judge it, that what one wanted the other could
scarcely refuse. I could tell of many glorious virtues of this Leger,
but since he still sails in uncertainty amidst the innumerable
storms of this life of earthly exile, human ignorance itself compels
me to keep silent, like it or not.[49] Not each who begins, but *he who
perseveres to the very end will be saved* [Mt 10:22]. Robert of happy memory sent a message to Leger, and with entreaties bid him to have
the kindness to come visit him. Having heard about Robert's illness, the faithful man hastened to see him.[50] After he arrived, he
ordered the little residence[51] to be guarded carefully day and night
by his servants, for he feared it would be deprived of such a great
patron, and accordingly commanded it to be well watched. Not
only did the archbishop of Bourges visit our Robert then, but also
several chief men of the region came to visit and ask after him.
Likewise they, too, carefully secured Orsan with their guards, remarking that they would be blessed indeed if they deserved to be
honored by such a great patron. Everyone who came to visit
Robert received a prize of comfort from him. For although weak
in body, still he took pains to distribute the salvific words of
preaching to the people around him in his accustomed way.

30. Meanwhile the messenger, who had been sent after the
abbess, came to La Puye.[52] Finding her there, he immediately di-
vulged why he had followed her and he urged her to come back to
Orsan with all speed. She and Angarde, who was with her, terribly
alarmed at such sad news, lost no time in departing and left La
Puye before dawn. At last they came to Orsan, sad and tearful. Ap-

proaching the still-living invalid, Petronilla cried out and said, "Alas, good Master! You will do no more good for us now!" But Angarde, who had come with her, gently scolded her. "Stop saying such things, good woman, and instead ask God that he deem it worthy even now to grant good health. He who has given Robert this illness will also provide for recovery when He pleases." Some still said that he would not die from this illness, but Robert himself declared otherwise.

31. It would take a long time to tell in detail how the wise, ailing man in his affliction was zealous to admonish visitors of each sex with salt-seasoned discourse [Col 4:6].[53] But because I do not want to bore my readers, I will pass to the things he did the third day before he died. On the fourth day before his death, he ordered Leger, the venerable archbishop of Bourges—who had come to see Robert, as we have said—to be called to him.[54] Robert said to him, "Oh dearest father, you are my archbishop, my primate and patriarch. You know how I have always up to now loved you and how I was obedient to you. You know too that I first came to these parts for love of you. You asked me to give some of my good women to you, and I did so. At your command and request I sent them to this province. As you know, I had then no houses, no possessions, no lands here. You made this place ready for them, for the salvation of your soul and the souls of your loved ones. With divine inspiration you built them this dwelling place, where they could perform God's service day and night. They brought with them no possessions, gold, silver, or even furnishings. You secured land, food and clothing, and all other things they needed; in both word and deed you rejoiced greatly at their arrival, and you have continued to honor them in many ways and to serve them well. Now: it is God's will that I am entering on the way of all flesh: *the time for my departure has come* [2 Tm 4:6] and I am no better than our fathers [1 Kgs 19:4]. Therefore while there is still breath in me, as long as I can speak, I commend my daughters, and everything that is theirs, to your affection, so that you, who bade them come here,

may piously watch over them, and be solicitous in caring for them from now on.

32. "Furthermore I want to tell your friendship my heart's desire; I want to reveal my desire to Your Holiness. If you ever loved me alive let it show as I die; let it be obvious if you ever held me dear, as you have said. You are not unaware that true love is not in words alone, but as Holy Scripture testifies, expression in good works is the proof of love: *Let us not love in word or speech, but in deed and truth* [1 Jn 3:18]. So I make it known to you, dearest Father, that I do not want to lie in Bethlehem, where God deigned to be born of a virgin, nor in Jerusalem at the Holy Sepulcher. Nor do I want to be buried in Rome among the holy martyrs, nor at the monastery of Cluny, where gorgeous processions take place.[55] I say these things not to disparage these holiest of places, because I know they truly ought to be loved, worshiped, and venerated out of reverence for the Lord's incarnation. All the faithful should greatly revere holy Bethlehem, a city praised by the prophets, worthy to be honored with the Lord's birth. Although God is everywhere, nevertheless everyone should lovingly honor holy Jerusalem with a certain distinction as the place in which the Son of God saw fit to redeem the world by his death. Nor should anyone scorn happy Rome, so red with the precious blood of such great martyrs that she exceeds all the beauty of the world, as Holy Scripture says.[56] Finally, what truly wise person would dare to slight the supreme monastery, Cluny, where every day there is such good service by God's grace?

33. "In the end I do not want to be buried anywhere other than Fontevraud. You know, my Father, that I made Fontevraud the head of all the other houses: the greater part of our flock, the foundation of our religious community, is there. I do not ask you to bury me in the monastery or in the cloister—just in the mud of Fontevraud among my little brothers.[57] There are my priests and clerics. There too are the holy virgins, widows, and chaste women, persevering day and night in praise of God. There are my very

beloved frail ones; there are my dearest lepers. There are the good companions of my wandering; those who long bore poverty and travail along with me for Christ's sake are there. There are those who patiently endured cold and heat, miseries and tribulations for the salvation of their souls, who at the words of my preaching left their homes and families with God's inspiration; some of them are still alive, others died persevering in obedience. There lies the nun Hersende, my good assistant, with whose advice and labor I raised the buildings at Fontevraud.[58] There lie my good sons whose prayers, I trust, intercede for me before God. There sleep my good nuns, by whose merits I believe I am aided before God. This is the reason, dearest Father, I decline burial in the holiest places: I want to be buried in the mud among my poor little brothers and sisters. For I know that while they were alive they wanted me to lie there so that on the day of Resurrection I would be able to go with them in this same flesh to God's judgment.

34. "If I am buried there, the living will love the place more, and those whom the Devil holds fast in disobedience will come to seek mercy. People will hear tell that I lie at Fontevraud and when they recall that God snatched them away from the worthless world [Gal 1:4] through me, and that he granted many goods to them through me, bound by love for me they will hasten to return to obedience. Who of my flock is so hard-hearted that he will not soften, groaning and sighing, when he fully remembers me? Thus when they call to mind how I always loved them, how I taught them, how God filled them with his precepts through me, by divine inspiration some of them, called forth by such favors and moved to penance, will come to seek God's mercy at my tomb. And because I feel this will happen, I commend to my posterity that they refuse the gift of pardon to no one in search of mercy. And if it please the Author of mercy that ever he deem it worthy to offer me anything—not according to my merit, about which I presume nothing, but through His undeserved kindness alone—I shall take pains to appeal continually to that very font of mercy for my whole congrega-

tion.[59] For there is no life here, here true love fails.[60] I will love them as I am able, since I will not be able to love them in this life. I know that no burial can harm the dead, and I believe without a doubt that the Lord can offer his aid everywhere to whom he wants. But all this I have said is the reason why I ask to lie there; this is the situation that causes me to direct my body to be buried in the cemetery at Fontevraud. Therefore I humbly beseech the reverence of Your Holiness to give my body to my nuns, and take it back to Fontevraud, and perform the office of burial there with your holy mouth. Soon it will show forth, at my death, if you ever truly loved me when I was alive.[61] Thus if you were my bosom friend, if I was ever a friend to you then I beg of you, grant me what I have asked."

35. The bishop, not wanting his diocese to be despoiled of such a treasure,[62] replied to Robert and said, "Dearest Master, I love you very much, with my whole being, as I have for a long time. Yet what you ask of me is not entirely in my power, but to a great extent belongs to the princes of this region. You know well that this place is in the territory of a certain prince named Alard, the one who built Orsan in large part. I do not want to make you any promises I cannot keep afterwards. But allow me to take counsel on this matter tomorrow."[63]

36. When he had heard this, the priest Andreas said to his master, "Good Master, your loving kindness knows that Agnes, the prioress of this place, can greatly help or hinder your request. So appeal to her that she do her part to fulfill your request; she is a native of this region, and Alard, the lord of this place, was her husband." So the wise Robert called her forth and said to her, "Oh Lady Agnes, I prayerfully command and commandingly pray you as my lady, my daughter, and my disciple: do whatever you can in this matter that I have asked the archbishop to arrange." She replied to him, "Good Master, you want me to do this?"[64] And he said, "I want this absolutely and desire it, daughter, and I bid you to kiss my hand to seal the agreement." Kissing his venerable hand, Agnes promised she would do what Robert's heart so desired.

37. After this, those present began to say, "O good Master, you should pray to God since you sense yourself so close to death." He replied to them, "I certainly very much desire to pray, but because of you, who thwart me, I cannot do so at all. Withdraw, go away, so I can at least pray to my God henceforth." When they had all gone, humbly he began to pray that God, in His mercy, would deign to maintain the Roman pope and all the teachers of His Holy Church in their resolution to live in religion to the very end.[65] Then he began to mention his hosts by name, and offer God a prayer for each one. Then he prayed for all his benefactors, for his enemies, and for all faithful people living and dead. Lastly he even began to beseech the Lord on behalf of Count William of Poitiers who was at that time, as he deserved, wounded by the sword of excommunication. Robert asked that if it was God's will, He might in His mercy call back William to the path of truth.[66] So it was evident how this man was filled with great love: right to the end he continued to pray for friends and foes with utmost devotion. It is quite clear that he loved his enemies as himself, since he hoped and prayed that what he desired from God would be given to them. Indeed, it is even plainer how wisely he loved the friends for whom he gently offered up the service of prayer to the Lord God. Let us describe, if we are able, the vigilance with which he observed the other mandates of the Law. He returned good for evil, which is usually most difficult; although he lay down to die in peace, according to God's will, nevertheless I believe he did not lose the martyr's palm.[67] And lest by chance what I say in any way displease, let any who object hear Holy Scripture confirm it, saying, "You accomplish martyrdom not just in the shedding of blood, but in forbearance from sins and in performance of God's commands." And again it is written: "Every life of a Christian is cross and martyrdom."[68]

38. After he had poured forth prayers to the Lord for all Christian people for a very long time, since nearly everyone had departed from him, in the silence of the dead of night he called to his side a certain lay brother named Peter, who was with him constant-

ly, and said to him, "Call the priest Andreas to me." When Andreas arrived, Robert said to him, "Bring me, I implore you, the wood of the holy cross." When the holy cross had been brought, full of joy he sprung up from his bed with as much strength as he could muster, and genuflected before it with great reverence, and conveyed to those present what he knew inwardly about God. Then Robert affirmed his belief that God omnipotent, the one in three and three in one, made heaven and earth and all that is in them [Ex 20:11] by the command of his will. Robert also professed that God placed in Paradise Lucifer, who rose in the morning, who is the beginning of the ways of God [Prv 8:22], bearing the sign of God's likeness, full of wisdom and beauty, adorned with every precious stone [Ezek 28:12]. He declared further how he believed that Lucifer fell voluntarily, without anyone's persuasion, through his own pride, and that as compensation, God wondrously made man in *his image and likeness* [Gn 1:26] *from the mud of the earth* [Gn 2:7]. Robert spoke about how death came into the world through the Devil's envy [Wis 2:24] and how the deceitful Enemy expelled man from Paradise. He called to mind how deep is the shadow of blindness and how many are the miseries the human race would bear until the end of the world because the first man disobeyed the Lord's command. To these remarks he added that the human race, as its sins warranted, perished in the waters of the flood, and how God saved eight souls in Noah's ark. He went on about how gloriously God freed the children of Israel from Egyptian enslavement and how wondrously, once the murmurers had died in the desert, he led the believers into the Promised Land.[69]

39. Prostrate before the holy cross, he told how the Son of God, descending into the womb of the Holy Virgin, made a new heaven and earth, just as he had promised [2 Pt 3:13], how He willed to be born in Bethlehem, placed in a manger, and wrapped in shabby rags for our salvation, not according to our merits, but by His mercy alone. He testified that not only did God deign to be made man for mankind's sake, but even more marvelous still, to be circum-

cised and baptized and to fast. Sighing, Robert recounted that the living bread who came down from heaven went hungry to satisfy us, that the living font thirsted to free us from eternal thirst. Groaning and sighing, Robert recounted that He who made all things by his will, made man for mankind's sake, stooped voluntarily to endure mocking and spit, blows from fists and whippings, insults and wounds, and in the end death on the cross—all for the redemption of mankind. The pious man also told about the Lord's resurrection and ascent to heaven and the coming of the Holy Spirit, and likewise added that the Lord would come again in judgment at the end of time, when God will mete out justice to each one according to his deserts.[70]

40. Finally Robert added that almighty God had caused him to be born of a little old man and a poor little woman, and how afterwards He had granted him innumerable blessings, through no merit of his own. After these things Robert poured forth thanksgiving to omnipotent God for these and other innumerable favors bestowed freely on the human race. Again, he gave God splendid thanks that He had afforded him such marvelous blessings, although through the merits of others.

41. After the Catholic man set out his beliefs in full before the holy cross and for those who stood listening, he proceeded to make public confession of his sins, accusing himself in an unheard-of manner, saying, "Priest, hear my sins; yea indeed, hear them, heaven and earth: the son of God *came into the world to save sinners, of whom I am the foremost* [1 Tm 1:15]. Behold: I was conceived in wickedness and nurtured in sins [Ps 50/51:7]. I have sinned by my own fault in countless ways." Then he confessed before all, berating himself that when he was a little boy and ate with his mother, he took the better portions, and when it rained he wanted it dry, and vice versa. He recalled, denouncing himself yet again, that while he was still of secular status he had once fallen in with the crime of simony in the election of a certain bishop of Rennes.[71] He further declared that God had freely given him great knowledge of litera-

ture and grace in preaching, and repented that he had not multiplied the talent entrusted him by God as he should have. Then
Robert said that he had gathered together religious communities
of women, who sustained excellently the labor of religious life for
God, but rued that he alone had gotten their praise.

42. Where is the space to tell it, if I wanted to relate one by one
how and in what ways Robert called himself to account before the
holy cross? After he had blamefully accused himself in an inde-
scribable way, naming each and every sin, he sought from God absolution for all his sins in humble supplication, and after that he
prayed for God to see fit to grant him death soon. It is certain that
God heeded His servant in prayer, since not long after these events
He loosed Robert from the chains of the flesh and removed him
from this world's exile.

[*Here begins the portion of Andreas's narrative preserved only in a French translation from ca. 1500. On this text, see the introduction to this* vita.]

Then after Robert, in no doubt about his plea, had finished his
prayers, he made a request of God, devoutly entrusting his family
to Him and saying, "O Father of mercy, I commend to you the
flock you committed to me, restoring them to Your holy care in order that You, who in the past have saved them from the wolves of
hell through my hands, will now keep them in all devotion to Your
holy service forever." When all this was finished, Robert ordered
his companions to return the cross to its place and all go to bed.
However, it is to be remarked here that not only once but three
times before his passing did he make his profession of faith in the
confession and prayers that we have noted above.

43. At midnight, while all his companions had gone to sleep, he
began to speak and say, "Woe to you, impious crowd! Why are you
here? *Withdraw from here* [1 Kgs 17:3]. *May the Lord rebuke you!* [Jude
1:9]"[72] And at this denunciation, Robert's convert, the lay brother
Peter, who was sleeping at his bedside, awoke and said to the good
father, "Until now I had hoped for your recovery, but since I see

that you are dreaming, I understand full well that you will die."
Then the good father replied to him, "And you think I dream, and
this is an illusion? No, no! It is not what you think." Hearing his
remark, the good lady, Sister Agnes,[73] utterly terrified, asked him,
"Alas, good father, what are you saying?" And he told her that it
was a throng of enemies who had come to trouble and terrify
him.[74] Making the sign of the cross, the good lady asked him if
they were still there. He answered that when he had raised his hand
and made the sign of the cross, they had all departed in silence.
Then the good lady questioned him again about how and in what
shape they had appeared. Robert told her that they were blacker
than coal and dressed like monks. Then she asked him, "How did
they dare come to you? Did they think they would find something
with which to reproach you?" "Surely," he replied, "they thought
that I should die like a beast and for that reason they came here, in
vain, to lie in wait and take advantage of me. For like it or not,
with God's help I shall die like a good Christian."

44. But one could ask here why the Enemy [i.e., Satan] appeared
in monastic habit, given that the said habit symbolizes penance
and that there is none of it in the Enemy, because he is always ob-
stinate in wickedness. To this the reply is that if we call to mind
what the Apostle said, that with God's permission, the Enemy
transforms himself into an angel of light [2 Cor 11:14], we shall not
be astonished. For he sometimes falsely takes on the penitential
habit in order that he might more easily deceive under the guise of
goodness and ruin wretched creatures. Moreover, one might ask
how the said enemies dared to draw near the death of so holy a
person. To this my lord St. Hilary replies that they are present at
the death of everyone, no matter how holy, as in the case of my
lord St. Martin.[75] Because the Enemy, by nature, can do no harm at
all to the good after their deaths, that is why he does not cease to
persecute them as long as they are in this world, more than ever at
the end, in order to frighten and trouble them. No wonder, then, if
at the end he wanted to harass a holy man by whom he had so

many times been vanquished and crushed in this world. So because during Robert's lifetime the Enemy had not been able to overcome him, thus he strove in every way possible to bring evil to bear on the dying man.

45. Who could possibly think how many souls Our Lord delivered from the power of the Enemy through Robert? And how many has Our Lord brought into His blessed realm through him? In truth, if we look faithfully at Robert's life and conduct, we will find nothing other than a constant battle against the Enemy. In him was born out what is written: "Be strong in warfare and fight the ancient serpent."[76] Who led more austere a life and persevered so long? At the beginning of his conversion he went two years without bread, eating only raw salted herbs.[77] Furthermore, during one period, he ate only once every three days and then only bread and water, in tears and weeping, moaning, often desiring to leave this unclean world. And all the rest of his life, he was above human nature, almost unbelievably able to tame his senses. Robert scorned the world and battled the Enemy in every way open to him. Afterwards, who could tell how he sacrificed himself in his heart before Our Lord when he wished to approach the altar's holy sacrament? Truly I can say with the prophet that he made burnt offering of marrow [Ps 65/66:15] and ate the true flesh of the immaculate lamb with wild lettuce [Nm 9:11]. For he knew well that a contrite and humble heart is most acceptable and welcome to God [Ps 50/51:19]. And so what do we wretched ones do at the end? If the Enemy wanted to obliterate and obstruct so holy a man, one of the principal lights of the Church, do we think in the least that he will not strive to obstruct and terrify us as much as he possibly can? For this reason, our only hope rests in the hand of Our Lord, through which He in His mercy will be able to deliver us from the Enemy's power.

46. Afterward, on the next day, Thursday, Alard, in whose territory Orsan lay and about whom we have spoken previously, came to the said good father because, in order to have his body carried

to Fontevraud, it was certainly necessary, and therefore Robert had bade him come.[78] When Robert saw him, he began, "My lord, my friend, you know how you and I have always loved one another. You are not unaware that I came to these parts, a poor preacher, and you received me, although undeserving, in friendship. You know, too, how at Fontevraud I gathered a great multitude of nuns who, owing to their number, could neither stay nor live together any longer, and furthermore how I searched for remote and deserted sites in which to settle and distribute them. And consequently you know that when I came to these parts, I was a stranger and had neither lands, nor houses, nor possessions here. Under the authority of your good archbishop Leger, for the salvation of your soul and those of your relations, you gave me this deserted place to build a little lodging for the handmaids of Jesus Christ. Then remember how I sent some of my brothers here to make the place ready and you helped them to build it. Afterwards, when the building was finished, by means of good prayers, the archbishop's and yours, I brought here some of my good nuns, for the love of whom you have even enlarged the place. You increased their lands and possessions, you gave gold and silver for their necessities, and up to the present you showed them signs of sincere love. Now, as it pleases Our Lord, I am about to pay the debt of nature. Indeed I know that you hold great sway in this land. For this reason, I pray you, see to it and help my disciples so that my body, after my death, be carried to the cemetery at Fontevraud. I know that the inhabitants of this land will want me to be buried here. But for myself, I do not want to be anywhere other than that cemetery at Fontevraud. Show in this way, after my death, that you loved me completely while I was alive. And if you do not want to do this for me alone, at very least do it for the love of your good wife, my dear daughter Sister Agnes, the prioress of this place."[79]

47. When the good lord Alard had heard this request, he replied to Robert that he completely loved him and his entire congregation, but that what Robert asked was hardly in his control, and

that he needed to speak first to the lords of Bourges, Raoul of Déols and Geoffrey of Issoudun.[80] After having heard their opinion, he would tell Robert what they thought. Then the good father summoned Abbess Petronilla, telling her that she should see to finding a litter, and have him carried back to Fontevraud while he was alive. For he saw well that his followers would struggle to keep his body. Alard told them that they should take care not to lay hands on Robert, and that people would say that they had caused him to die through their greed and thus they would be less esteemed by the world.[81]

48. So the good father spoke again to the aforementioned Alard. "You know how I founded Fontevraud as the head of my entire order and had it confirmed from Rome by grant of Pope Pascal.[82] But now the end of my earthly pilgrimage is at hand and I know that my holy household will have much to suffer for possession of my body. For this reason, because you have great power in these parts, if you would promise me that you will help my disciples insofar as you are able, I will do what you wish." Then the good lord Alard promised that however much it might grieve him, he would have Robert taken as far as the land of the count of Anjou, and as proof of this he gave Robert his hand, saying to Petronilla that it would be necessary to beseech that same count, and that it would cause great misfortune, after Robert died in their own land, that others not of their land should have the consolation for it.[83]

49. Afterwards the good father said to the abbess and the whole congregation, "As many times as people oppose you, still do not give up! Although I do not wish it for my own sake, send messengers to Rome and do not depend on good will toward Fontevraud. Take on neither battle nor quarrel, for I forbid it, for obedience's sake. But I command you only to do what you are able, without cost to the mother house. For if you persist, you will carry me back to Fontevraud." At this juncture, the whole convent arranged to come visit Robert. When they had arrived, they began to weep

tenderly, complaining and saying, "Alas, our good father, very soon you will leave us desolate orphans." Then he began to console them, telling them that they should always persevere in their good way of life. Seeing young girls so tearful and afflicted surrounding him, he began to caress them with his hand and soothe them, saying, "Alas, my children, I have prayed to Our Lord that it please him to deliver me from this world. But if such was His pleasure, I would still be happy to nourish and teach you, still ready to endure and suffer out of love for you." Oh kindness! Oh perfect love! Oh great and inestimable charity, after the holy man had labored, borne, and endured so much, following the example of my lord St. Martin, who said, "I am prepared for the work of His household, as long as he orders me to serve."[84] In truth it is clearly evident in this how ardently Robert desired to contemplate his Creator; however, seeing his troop so downcast, charity constrained him and he did not want to refuse the still necessary service to his family. For he knew that whoever is able to come to the rescue of those in danger and does not do it is not without fault.

50. Afterward he began to admonish them, as was his custom, to walk in virtue, entrusting himself to their good prayers after his death. And he explained that for love of them, he had often put aside his way of life in order to help them. Indeed, God's mercy always going before him and following after him, he would have lived excellently in religion if divine pity had not constrained him to come to the aid of their weakness. For on his own he had left all possessions and worldly honors and chosen to lead an utterly solitary life and inhabit the wilderness, in hunger and nakedness, so that he might overcome the tumult of this world—as it is written: *Behold, I fled and went a long way off, and I remained in solitude* [Ps 54/55:8]. He also chose always to wear a hairshirt and go barefoot to preach the Word of God and content himself only that listeners be given to him that they might welcome what his nature had finally demanded, thereby conforming to the divine commandment: *The laborer is worthy of his wage* [Lk 10:7; 1 Tm 5:18]. And so, whenever he

found himself in a suitable place, he strove to scatter the divine Word by day and then retired to deserted places to pray to God at night. And in this fashion he lived a life of contemplation and action in such a way that he was an indomitable stifler of vices and a powerful sower of virtues, such that he said he would have ended his days in this way if charity had not compelled him to do otherwise.[85]

51. When the next day came, Friday, it seemed that he was no better and his last day was at hand, which day, according to poetic stories, is called *veneris* by syncope, that is, venerable.[86] For all the faithful it is a day of veneration because on it the Savior of the world was crucified and redeemed us with His own blood. Then all the brothers assembled before him and said, "Alas, our good father, we see clearly now that you are leaving us. Therefore we pray you, before your demise, to teach us what we have to do." He replied, "Surely, my brothers, if for a long time I had not taught you how you should live and what you should do, it would be far too late now. You know perfectly well that I have always told you to do good and turn from sin [1 Pt 3:11]. You know the precepts I have given you: do these things and you will be saved [Sir 3:2]. You also know that I have commanded you to obey the handmaids of Jesus Christ throughout your entire lives, for the salvation of your souls, and to serve them out of love of their bridegroom Jesus, and you will be rewarded for it in the blessed realm of Paradise." This reminder finished, he sent them away.

52. Afterwards he summoned the Abbess Petronilla and Angarde, who had left their abbey to follow him, and Sister Agnes, prioress of Orsan, who with the permission of her husband Alard became a nun. Then he said to them, "My daughters, you know there is no creature on earth that does not die, because *He made the decree and will not change it* [Ps 148:6].[87] And as of necessity I am departing, ask me anything you wish to consult about now because I shall not speak to you further." In weeping and in tears they said to him, "Alas, our good father and pastor, teach us now how we

should live after your death and how we ought to keep our rule."
He replied: "Preserve the worthiness of your religious practice as
you have begun it and do not move either to the right or to the left
[Prv 4:27]. Strive to grow from strength to strength [Ps 83/84:8].
For as it is written: There can be no retreat from advance,[88] because
the path to Paradise is narrow and the wide and spacious road
leads to Hell [Mt 7:13–14]. And finally: if you wish to do anything
new, never do it without the counsel of your religious brothers."[89]

53. These good ladies thus consoled, Brother Andreas, his chaplain, came to his side, and when Robert saw him he said, "Surely I
can talk no longer and my senses fail. So hasten to ask me what
you want." Then he began to pray, saying, "Christ Jesus, son of the
living God, have mercy on me! Holy Mother of God, help me! All
the holy angels and archangels of God, pray for me! Every saint of
God, have mercy on me!" And when he had finished this prayer, he
fell silent. So Brother Andreas took up the holy taper and seeing
that Robert's face was changing and he had fainted, he began to
weep aloud. The priest hurriedly assembled all the brothers and
sisters who had come in such great number to visit Robert.

54. As soon as they had come, lamenting they said, "Alas! Alas,
our good father and pastor, as it pleases Our Lord, you are going
to Paradise and leaving us wards and orphans in this earthly pilgrimage. And because we are so feeble with our many sins, please
give us your blessing and absolution." Then Robert began to say
the *Confiteor* and gave them the customary ecclesiastical absolution.
And then he ordered them to chant the *Pater Noster* as their
penance.[90] Then he said, "Brothers and sisters, I commend my
body and soul to almighty God, the blessed Virgin Mary and all
the saints, and to your pious prayers." And thus, making the sign of
the holy cross for himself and for his flock, amidst the tears of his
brothers and the lamentations of his nuns, he died and gave over
his devout soul to Our Lord on that Friday at the hour of Vespers.
And as we piously believe, his happy soul flew away to heaven.

55. When the assembled company saw that the holy man had

died, they wished to keep his passing a secret. But because the magnitude of their grief did not admit of any limit to their tears, although they wanted to keep from crying, the more they took care to hold back tears, the more they wept. Then they took the body from the private room and carried it, fully dressed, to the nuns' cloister, for fear that someone might take it from them. Then the servants of the lords of Bourges, Alard and [Geoffrey of] Issoudun, who kept watch at Orsan, seeing the holy household weeping so, went quickly and burst through the sisters' gates to seize the body and carry it to the chapel where the good archbishop was, until such time as he ordered and declared what would be done with it.[91] But because Robert's body was not yet shrouded, all the brothers and sisters asked first that they be able to enshroud him.

56. On Saturday, the brothers readied him for burial and dressed him in hairshirt and robe, seeing that they could by no other means fend off such a crowd of laymen. Then they placed him in a coffin, laboring to perform a funeral. But God knows "how great was the mourning of all"[92] bewailing together the loss of their pious father, since a choir of his daughters wept while singing of it and sang while weeping. For the love of him, and the grief that filled them, they could not in any way be consoled. That day and night they did not rest, nor drink, nor eat.

57. Alas! Who could properly express here the pity and grief of this poor company? Some women beat their breasts, moaning tenderly; others cried aloud, indescribably; still others collapsed prostrate on the ground. People came from everywhere and nearly the whole city of Bourges assembled at Orsan. Some wept and rejoiced—the first because they mourned the loss of such a good teacher, the second because God had adorned their diocese with such a saintly personage who, as they believe, would intercede for them in Paradise. Seeing the rush of people, Petronilla prostrated herself and she and her flock wept at the feet of the powerful ones, asking that they might plead with the lord archbishop of Bourges

that he take pity on them and Fontevraud and leave them in peace to take their father and patron back to the said Fontevraud.

58. Then, when the good archbishop heard this, he told them he would take counsel with his clergy on the matter and give his answer the next day, Sunday. On Saturday, the good archbishop had made a handsome stone coffin for the body of the holy man, his good friend. Then he called together a great multitude of abbots, clerics, nobles, and laypeople and asked their opinion: should he let them carry the body of the good father to Fontevraud in peace, or have him buried at Orsan? After having heard their advice, he sent some lords of the region to Petronilla and her flock with the bishop's word—they should leave in peace the good father's body that was given to them by the grace of God, so they could perform funeral rites honorably and triumphantly and bury him there at Orsan, a daughter house of Fontevraud, after all. For if God had wanted Robert to be buried at Fontevraud, he would not have allowed him to die in these parts. "It should suffice for them," the bishop declared, "that they knew his counsel and intimate company more than any others living, and it is fitting they allow him to us in death, since we had him so rarely during his lifetime."[93]

59. When they heard this, the good abbess Petronilla and her followers were extremely frightened. The good lady replied to the bishop's messengers that she would in no way concede, and that she would bring the matter before the papal legate and to the curia at Rome, and that if nobody wished to do right by her she would appeal to God, the true Judge of all, concerning the harm they wanted to do. For the judgment he deserves is rendered to every person as befits him and so there is no pope, king, prince, or person so powerful that the Judge of fairness will not do justice concerning him. The lords who had been sent, hearing this woman's response, were quite taken aback and returned to the lord bishop of Bourges and told him what the good abbess had said. Then they said to him, "Reverend father, know that we will no longer interfere in this affair, for we do not in the least want to be accused be-

fore God on this count. This ecclesiastical matter is out of our jurisdiction, for we are laymen and should not place our hand on the Lord's anointed, just as it is written: *Do not touch my anointed ones* [1 Chr 16:22]. As for you, you are the archbishop: sacerdotal and spiritual care is entrusted to you. As such, wisely consider what you must do so that on Judgment Day you will not be scolded or rebuked about it." Having said these things, all departed. When the lords had left, some of the bishop's servants came to him and said, "My lord, permit us to carry him to Bourges, and that way you will be without opposition." The good prelate, hearing all these things, was in doubt about what he should do. Meanwhile, a pious funeral took place in the nun's cloister and laymen stood watch over the body in this spirit: they were more upset about their unjust desire to detain the holy man than they were about his death.[94]

60. Afterwards, when Monday came, the nuns, in the increase of their grief and to pacify the good archbishop, made a procession around the precinct of their cloister, all of them barefoot and without their cloaks, that is, wearing nothing but their black habits and veils.[95] All weeping, they went to prostrate themselves before the holy body and vowed that they would never drink nor eat until the holy man had succeeded in having his body carried to Fontevraud.[96]

61. When the servants of the lord bishop of Bourges who were keeping watch by the tomb saw and heard these wondrous doings, some of them, filled with sorrow, went back to their master and told him what the nuns had done. The good archbishop, moved by pity, came to the nuns and said to them, "Alas, my dear daughters, I thought you loved your good master, but now I know the contrary is true. You know how I gave of myself to you and how I love this place, even how I have chosen to be buried here. I rejoiced greatly that God had given me such a companion as Robert, and wanted to keep him so I could be buried at his feet. It is certainly my view that you should be quite content and desire that he remain here at Orsan in order that, through his merits, Our Lord would wish to increase this, your present place. So put off your

sadness and put on your cloaks and drink and eat as you have been accustomed. Without eating you cannot live, and fasting will excuse you for sinning. You know you have no reason to bewail the holy man, for all must die, but the death of a righteous man is most precious to Our Lord, as it is written: *Blessed are the dead who die in the Lord* [Rv 14:13]. Furthermore, you are not unaware that our good friend lived virtuously on earth. Now we believe he lives and reigns in heaven more joyfully. Therefore take off and discard your grief, rejoice in his blessed consolation, and pray Our Lord that it please Him to inspire me about what I must do."

62. The nuns replied, "Certainly we are no longer your daughters and we will no longer pray for you and yours until you return our good father to us. Know this: if he had wanted to be buried here he would not have directed us otherwise, nor entreated you to have him carried to Fontevraud and to perform the funeral there yourself! How can we show that we are his daughters if we do not fulfill his commands?" And the good archbishop, hearing this reply, went away very sad [Mt 19:22].[97]

63. When Tuesday came, the archbishop summoned Petronilla along with some of her sisters and brothers and said to them, "I see clearly that you are still determined in your purpose and will not be comforted if you do not get what you ask. I tell you: the compassion I have for you constrains me. I bear witness before God: what I have done was for nothing other than the love I bore for Robert, and I very much wanted him buried here so I could be placed at his feet. I believe that it would have profited me to be accompanied by such a holy personage before Our Lord. Therefore, pardon me and mine for what we have done and the pain we have caused you. Stay again today and tomorrow you will depart under the protection of Our Lord. And just as your good master beseeched and requested of me, with God's help I will go and perform the funeral myself." At this, the good mother abbess and all those with her prostrated themselves at his feet, humbly thanking him.

64. Then, the next day, they left to take him to Fontevraud. And

although every one of them was greatly grieved and distressed at the death of their good father, nonetheless they rejoiced greatly to carry him back to Fontevraud. Marvel! None of them could keep from weeping; however, they admonished one another to restrain themselves and take comfort, and whoever could not take comfort from another offered succor to the others through tearful prayers.

65. On the following Sunday, all the brothers of Fontevraud and also all the people of the town, from the least to the greatest, walked alongside the body for about one league, everyone barefoot and bare-headed, in weeping and tears.[98] All also rejoiced in the assurance that they would take charge of their good father's bier and coffin. But there arrived as well the men of Candes, peaceful enemies, who wanted to carry Robert to [the church of] St. Martin and said that it would be fitting, because they had been friends and neighbors, that they be consoled in doing Robert's service and obsequies, at very least for one night.[99] The male and female religious saw that the request came not in entreaties but rather something more like threats. Considering the troubles they had had at Orsan and fearing difficulty, they did not want to trust anyone. Then the men of Candes insisted to the point of harming, striking, and hurting religious men and women. This attack notwithstanding, the people of Fontevraud, scorning their injuries and the danger, kept along through the fields in prayers and orisons—by which they were more victorious than the people of Candes with their swords and cudgels. Seeing that their hope was in vain, the latter went along with the company to Fontevraud and once there begged pardon for the evil they had done, saying they would not have behaved so but for their love of the holy man and with good intent.

66. Afterwards, when they had arrived at Fontevraud, the body was carried for the first night into the Great Monastery in the sisters' cloister. The nuns performed his service all night in prayers, orisons, and tears. The next day, they took him to St. Lazarus, since while alive he had served and ministered to the inhabitants in great devotion. For this cause, it made good sense that they espe-

cially have the consolation of performing his service.[100] Then, they took him to the Madeleine, and those there did likewise.[101] When the next day came—in order to satisfy not only the crowd of neighbors who had come to see him, but also innumerable people who had come from various regions, as many laymen as religious and of all stations—he was taken from the Madeleine to the square in front of the main abbey church and there shown to all to repay their devotion somewhat.

67. Meanwhile, the brothers arranged the place, discussing where exactly they should lay him to rest. Although he had instructed that he be buried in the cemetery with his good religious men and women, still a number of archbishops and bishops, abbots and monks, nobles and great lords who were present[102] said that he should be buried in the main church, given that he had been its founder and, all his life, its guardian and defender and protector as well as an evangelical preacher. "As many times as he had said that he wanted to be in the cemetery, the request came only of his humility, and moreover, since he had right to the end so adorned this church, there was good cause for him to be honored in this fashion. For, as St. Gregory said, just as being buried in holy places harms the wicked, so too does it benefit the good."[103]

68. And so with all things well and duly ordered, bathed in tears they carried the body of the holy man and placed it to the right of the great altar of Fontevraud. Because the good metropolitan archbishop of Bourges was the most esteemed of the company in worthiness and holiness, with due reverence he performed the burial office, as he had promised his good friend when alive. The day of Robert's burial was the twelfth after his decease, that is, Tuesday, at the hour of Vespers.[104] The holy man buried, each mourner arranged for departure. The next day, the reverend Father gave a sermon in the brothers' chapter house and gave his blessing to them and to all the nuns.[105] Then he took his leave of the whole congregation, commending himself to their good prayers.

69. And now it is time to render thanks to Our Lord and to

praise, if it is permitted, the holy conduct of our good father and pastor. Let us extol our royal leader after his triumph! Let us now praise his good fortune, because I believe, I hope, and I trust that having navigated the surging storms of this earthly exile, he has now arrived at the port of salvation. And so now he has firmly cast his anchor and, by the grace of Our Lord, has docked his ship laden with precious goods at the desired port. Certainly in his lifetime it was very necessary; how much more it would be now! For day by day love grows cold and wickedness abounds [Mt 24:12] according to the saying of the prophet: *There is no truth, no mercy, no knowledge of God in the land, but it overflows with wickedness, lying, murder, thieving, and adultery, and bloodshed follows on bloodshed* [Hos 4:1–2]. He was the blameless salt of the earth and light of the world [Mt 5:13–14]. As the Apostle said, for some the smell of life, for others the smell of death [2 Cor 2:16]. Truly he was greater than Joseph in patience and greater than Moses in delivering sinners from servitude to the Enemy. For in the wilderness he was a very powerful leader, showing the way to the true Promised Land in his life and teaching. Without a doubt he was a true Daniel in wisdom, a Samuel in justice and mercy. Following the example of the herald of Our Lord, he spent most of his life in the desert, contenting himself with herbs and water and a very rough hairshirt.[106] Truly he was John the Baptist in the desert in his life and preaching, Arsenius in his prayer and weeping, Martha in his welcome and service, Paul in his preaching and travel.[107] And before he could reach Paradise, from the time of his conversion he always went from strength to strength [Ps 83/84:8] and forgot and abandoned the world in order to do good day by day.

70. Surely he was a person adorned with beauty, cheerful of face, delightful in love, austere in the honor of his ways, discreet in his works, generous in mercy, zealous in obedience, humble in teaching, faithful in promises, assiduous in learning, dazzling in speech, admirable in wisdom, moist-eyed, the elect and chosen of God in preaching. Because of the way he lived in religion, he was the sup-

port of the lame, the eye of the blind [Jb 29:15], the comfort of the
forsaken, a father to orphans, a spouse of holy widows, a guardian
and protector of virgins, a refuge for the wretched, a planter of
virtues, an eradicator of vices, a harmonizer of discords, love of
the hateful, peace of the belligerent—all this through the ardor
that was in Him with whom Robert was filled.

71. Who is there capable of telling how many times Robert, by
the grace of Our Lord, restored peace between kings, counts, and
princes quarreling and just at the point of entering into battle with
one another? Or how often he pacified lords of the Church at odds
with each other? Moreover, in all his deeds he showed himself a
true Christian, as was evident one day when he was in Auvergne.
He came to a place called Menelay l'Abbaye, armed with the fervor
of faith, to preach in this monastery.[108] The people of the country
told him that women could not go in the church, and if any one of
them presumed to enter, she would die at once. Learning this, the
Lord's good servant, since he wanted to go and preach, led in several women, against the will of those who stood watch at the doors,
and showed them before all present that their lies were impious.
Then the doorkeepers began devoutly to beg St. Menelay, and to
cry aloud that it should please him to take vengeance on such presumption, scorn, and insult.

72. Rich in spirit and discernment, the holy man replied, "Alas,
simple people, do not continue such foolish prayers in vain! Know
instead that the saints are not the enemies of the brides of Jesus
Christ. For what you are saying is absurd and the purity of the
Catholic faith clearly says the opposite—as it is written in the
Gospel concerning the blessed sinful woman who kissed the feet
of the Redeemer, washed them with her tears, dried them with
her hair, and poured ointment on His very worthy head [Lk
7:36–50].[109] And so who dares to say that there should be any
church into which a woman is not permitted entry, if she not be
forbidden by reason of faults and sins? Which is the greater thing,
God's material temple or the spiritual temple in which God lives [1

Cor 3:16–17]? If a woman takes and eats the body and blood of Jesus Christ, think what folly it is to believe that she may not enter a church." After he had shown the truth, this wrong ceased and totally perished.

Around this same time he went to Gascony, to a city called Agen, and there he persecuted and denounced numerous heretics. Nevertheless, because they did not want to convert and return to the faith, he had them removed from the community of the Church.[110]

[73. After these things I very much want to add what happened afterwards.[111] I learned in the *Life of Bernard of Tiron* about the good and worthy acts Robert saw. In the times of Pope Pascal II, Philip, the first king of France by that name, repudiated his own wife and took instead Bertrade, the wife of Count Fulk of Anjou.[112] When the pope heard of it, on this account he sent to France a legate named John and gave him as a companion one Benedict, greatly esteemed for authority and learning. When they arrived in Poitiers, the two legates summoned a great assembly of bishops, abbots, nobles, and numerous other notable people. When the king was alerted, he immediately sent a herald to William, the duke of Aquitaine, with the message that he should not allow the pope to do him such an injury in his own city of Poitiers.

74. When the duke had heard the news, to obey his king he went to the council to say that they should not be so bold to conspire against the king, or he would have them all beheaded. Nevertheless, the holy man Master Robert, fearing more to offend the eternal King than Philip, the temporal king, stood still as a column and much like the tower of David [Song 4:4],[113] surrounded and accompanied by three good men—Bernard of Tiron, Pierre de l'Etoile, abbot of Fontgombaud, and William of Nevers, of whom we have already spoken.[114] The four stood firm and pursued the case against the king to the end, with the result that they returned his own wife Bertha to the king and took away Bertrade, the count's wife, with her two illegitimate children by Philip. Then

they enclosed Bertrade at Hautes-Bruyères and there she did her penance and endowed the house with numerous goods.[115] Upon her death, she had herself buried there in the nave, in the middle of the sisters' choir. This story shows clearly that the holy man, Master Robert, would have freely suffered martyrdom for Our Lord, if the opportunity had presented itself.]

75. For he was surely a man who, by the grace of Our Lord, did a great deal in little time. We believe his soul was so pleasing to God, as it is written, that Our Lord wanted to take him out of this world in order to converse with him. And because in his lifetime Robert tried with all his might to please Our Lord, He took him away from this unclean world [Gal 1:4] not worthy of such a person. As my lord St. Gregory says, "The wickedness of the worldly often deserves the punishment that those who could do good are soon taken away from us here. The closer the end of the world, the more quickly the chosen are taken away for fear that they should see the evils carried out day by day."[116] The truth of this was very clearly shown to us after the death of the aforementioned good father, for if we are very sad at his passing, nonetheless we rejoice that he has evaded the snares of the Enemy and that he lives and reigns now with Jesus Christ. And since out of love for Him Robert mortified his flesh and overcame his vices and desires, now he is rewarded in Paradise. We have lost our comforter, but we have gained him as our helper; we have lost our good father and pastor, but oh, how much more now is he our advocate before the Creator. We have lost our counselor, but oh, how we hope he is our supplicant before God with the blessing of Jesus Christ, to whom be honor, praise, and glory eternal.

Amen! Amen! Amen! Thanks be to God!

ROBERT OF ARBRISSEL'S WRITINGS

1. Exhortation to the Countess of Brittany (1109)

Since preaching was Robert's final and longest-lived calling, the focus of his life from the mid-1090s to his death, it is fitting that the longest surviving document in his name is a sort of sermon. The twelfth-century manuscript in which it survives entitles it *Sermo domni Roberti de Arbruessello ad comitissam Britanniae*, "Lord Robert of Arbrissel's Sermon to the Countess of Brittany." But this is not a transcript of one of the public addresses for which Robert was famed. In form it is more like a letter, and is often referred to as such. Its contents are essentially advice to a privileged woman on how to fuse Christian practices and ideals with a busy life in the aristocratic milieu. It is, then, a somewhat unusual text, but one that provides a glimpse of Robert's rhetorical technique and poses questions both about his mission and about his views of Christian institutions and people.

The countess was the extraordinary Ermengarde, daughter of Count Fulk IV of Anjou. Born shortly before 1070, she appears to have been engaged to the future Duke William IX of Aquitaine, but the marriage was probably never consummated. By the mid-1090s Ermengarde was married to Count Alan IV of Brittany (1084–1119). The local poet-bishop Marbode of Rennes, who delivered a scathing critique of Robert translated below, wrote a poem in praise of Ermengarde's beauty and character, calling her powerfully eloquent and extremely astute (*pollens eloquio, callida con-*

silio), the glory of Brittany (*decus Armoricae regionis*). Ermengarde was regent over Brittany from 1096 to 1101, ruling capably during the nearly five-year absence of her husband on crusade.

Ermengarde's marriage took her from the sophisticated world of her father's court, centered in Angers, to the far rougher society to the northwest, in a region that Baudri of Dol, in his *vita* of Robert of Arbrissel, called the land of scorpions, and that Marbode, a native of Anjou made bishop of Rennes in 1096, scorned for its lack of culture. In addition the union was, like nearly all aristocratic marriages of this era, an alliance of family interests rather than mutually attracted individuals, in this case a way to join Brittany and Anjou in common cause against the powerful rulers of nearby Normandy. Ermengarde became restless after some years and the birth of three children. As Robert's letter shows, she sought an end to her marriage through flight and appeal to an ecclesiastical court but failed to get the desired annulment. It was shortly afterward, in 1109, that Robert wrote to her. In 1112, her husband retired to Redon, a monastery in Brittany. It has been suggested that Ermengarde spent time at Fontevraud either before Robert's letter or after her husband's retirement, but there is no contemporary evidence of any such sojourns. The exact nature of Robert and Ermengarde's relationship is uncertain. It is hardly surprising, however, that a famous preacher from Brittany who spent much time in Anjou would be known to the daughter and wife of the leading men of those regions.

Count Alan renounced all political authority a few years after he went to Redon. Ermengarde was an influential figure in the court of her son, the new count, for the next fifteen years. In about 1130, Ermengarde came under the influence of Bernard of Clairvaux, the most celebrated monk of his time and a speaker of power comparable to Robert. Two affectionate letters from Bernard to the countess have survived. Following Bernard to his native Burgundy, she decided to become a nun and entered a monastery there. Shortly afterward, Ermengarde set out in the company of a

few nuns for the Holy Land. There her brother, Count Fulk V of
Anjou, had become King of Jerusalem, the title given the lord of
territory in the eastern Mediterranean seized by European cru-
saders. After a few years in the East, Ermengarde returned to Brittany to resume life in the court, in which she remained active until
a few months before her death in 1147.

The present text, though, tells us less about its recipient than its
author. The closest thing to transcriptions of Robert's discourses
are in Andreas's *vita*. This is not surprising. Most sermons that have
survived from the twelfth century or before were designed for a
monastic audience, preserved as they were delivered: in Latin, the
language of the educated elite. Since the times of Charlemagne,
preachers had been encouraged to speak in the native language of
their audience, but only in Robert's lifetime had Europeans begun
to write in these everyday spoken languages, or "vernaculars."
(Robert's adversary and Ermengarde's one-time fiancé, William IX
of Aquitaine, wrote some of the earliest surviving lyric poetry in a
European vernacular.) Until long after Robert's death, even sermons given in the language of common people were preserved
only in Latin versions. Nothing at all by Robert's contemporary
hermit-preachers Bernard of Tiron and Vitalis of Savigny has survived, but the fortunate preservation of the *Sermo* can give some
notion of the message and technique that made Robert so
renowned.

Robert weaves several themes into his advice to Ermengarde on
how to live a holy life in the world. He begins with the offense of
hypocrisy and the need for moderation and caution in spiritual
pursuits. Robert is critical in several places of people who pretend
to please God while acting to please men, specifically the simoniacal and hypocritical clergy and mendacious, sexually degenerate
laypeople among whom Ermengarde finds herself. If Robert is to
be believed, the moral character and behavior of clergy in Brittany
had not much improved since his days as archpriest of Rennes
twenty years earlier. He is attentive to Ermengarde's marital disap-

pointment (and by implication to the general circumstances of elite marriage) but, forbidding any rebellion against authority, encourages a religious regimen according to the possibilities of her situation. She is to pray numerous times daily, persevere in the face of Christ's enemies and their hatred, give alms to the poor, and in all things exercise caution and discretion. Her ultimate reward will repay the difficulties of such a life.

What makes this exhortation most like a sermon is its abundant quotation of and allusion to Christian scripture. In only a few pages, there are dozens of biblical quotations and paraphrases, plus numerous additional references to biblical figures or events. The density of citations is typical of medieval monastic sermons and study: readers and writers, steeped in the Bible, tended to recall one passage, then another to which it is connected by a word or theme or textual affiliation, then another, and so on—a kind of mental hyperlink system by which readers and speakers "surfed" the Bible for their own enlightenment and that of their audience. For monastic readers, then, reading (often done aloud) was inseparable from meditation and prayer. Exegesis, or commentary, proceeded via this process of memory and connection rather than in what we would call systematic scrutiny. Robert's letter to Ermengarde is an instance of this meditative approach to scripture, aimed less at analysis or "learning" than at contemplation and salvation. In section 2, a mention of law leads to three citations on true justice, one from Leviticus, the third book of the Old Testament, one from John's Gospel, and one from the New Testament letter-sermon of James. In sections 6 and 7, Robert recalls the Psalms ten times in a row. In section 8 he gives a rapid succession of eleven examples of God's protection of his faithful servants culled from several books of the Old Testament. He cites Jesus' Sermon on the Mount (Matthew 5–7) some twenty times. Throughout, Robert uses biblical language and examples to illustrate and amplify his message. His technique of biblical study and reference is not that of the cathedral schools in which he studied, but a more meditative and nonlinear process suited to a hermit.

Especially striking in view of Robert's encouragement of monasticism and sheltering of women who desired to leave a life in the world for one in religion, Robert does not recommend dramatic change to Ermengarde. Instead he encourages her, having returned to her husband in obedience to ecclesiastical decree, to foster private and interior piety and spirituality through patient endurance, charity, and scorn of worldly pleasures and vanities. He stresses the three so-called "theological virtues" of faith, hope, and love (after 1 Corinthians 13), trust in God, and appropriate expressions of faith, for the latter drawing heavily on Matthew 6, the central portion of the Sermon on the Mount. However, Robert returns at the end to the need for moderation in spiritual practice. In short, he does not sanction the kind of uncompromising aspiration and rigor for which he and his followers were known. Nor does he encourage Ermengarde to flee her husband, something for which he had, rightly or not, a reputation: a few years after Robert died, the Parisian scholar Roscelin remembered him as a man who had "disobediently and to the death" refused to return unhappy wives to the husbands they had left. The message here is one of hope, God's love, and the need for patient accommodation with the demands of this world. Perhaps it was these ideas that characterized Robert's preaching.

In the end, though, some of Robert's intentions and opinions remain opaque. It is perhaps only coincidence that this one surviving sample of his distinctive eloquence is addressed to a woman. Did Robert recognize in Ermengarde another restless soul and think it better that she be tamed? Is that because she was a member of the titled nobility, or because she was a woman? Are his remarks on her marital situation comforting, or even meant to be so? One wonders if Robert would have made the same recommendations to an unhappy husband. His comments on Alan, whom he describes as *infidelis*, an infidel or faithless, are curious in light of the count's service in holy war, his sponsorship of ecclesiastical reform, his patronage of monasteries, and his retirement to Redon only a few years later. What had Robert heard, or what had Ermengarde told him? Finally, Robert's attitude toward the institutional Church is very hard to gauge. He urges obedience to authorities and at the same time is highly critical of the simony and hypocrisy of the clergy; he champions orthodoxy but enters, as a male cleric, into intimate dialogue with a laywoman. Such apparent contradictions made Robert a troubling figure even in his lifetime.

TEXT: Jean de Pétigny, "Lettre inédite de Robert d'Arbrissel à la comtesse Ermengarde," *Bibliothèque de l'Ecole des Chartes* 15 (1854): 225–235

1. The spirit of pride is bad, but the pretense of humility is worse. The spirit of vainglory is bad, but the pretense of sanctity is worse. The spirit of envy is bad, but the pretense of love is worse. The spirit of greed is bad, but the pretense of mercy is worse. The spirit of gluttony is bad, but the pretense of abstinence is worse. The spirit of lust is bad, but the pretense of chastity is worse.[1] Handmaid of Christ: beware these evils heard and known, manifest or pretended. For virtue is the middle ground between vices. See that you do nothing to excess: everything excessive is turned into vice.

2. Do not trust or yield to every spirit [1 Jn 4:1]. There are certain people *adulterating the Word of God* [2 Cor 2:17], desiring to please not God but men and who pervert the Scriptures to their own wicked will, not judging according to the Gospel and decrees and holy laws as it is written: *Judge not by appearance, but judge with just judgment* [Jn 7:24].[2] James says: *If you show favoritism, you commit sin, convicted by the law* [Jas 2:9]. As it is written: *You should not consider the rank of the poor, nor honor the countenance of the powerful; judge your neighbor justly* [Lv 19:15]. Others, very simple and rash, ignorant of the power of God's words (which are sometimes said allegorically, sometimes preceptively)[3] dispute about the Gospel and against it. They say that the Lord has forbidden us to be angry and to say Raca and

fool [Mt 5:22], that He taught us to offer the other cheek to him striking us [Mt 5:39], that He absolutely forbade us to take up lawsuits and ordered us to offer our cloak to one taking away our tunic [Mt 5:40], and told us to love our enemies and *pray for those who persecute us* [Mt 5:44] and to *do unto others whatever you want them to do unto you: this is the law and the prophets* [Mt 7:12].[4] They declare that it is against the Gospel and the Laws and the prophets even to do justice, whether by corporal punishment, confiscation of property, or any other harsh penalty without considering what is written in the Law: *Do not allow evildoers and murderers to live* [Ex 22:18]. To punish murderers and adulterers, rapists and wicked men of this kind is not bloodshed, but the dictate of Law. And, as St. Augustine says, does it not put many people in danger to spare such crimes?[5] Again a prophet speaks: God seeks from us nothing other than that we love justice and exercise mercy [Mi 6:8]. For if justice does not go first, peace does not follow [Ps 33/34:15, 1 Pt 3:11]. *Blessed are those who keep right justice and do justice rightly at all times* [Ps 105/106:3]. And in the Gospel: *Blessed are those who hunger and thirst for justice* [Mt 5:6], and likewise: *Blessed are those who suffer persecution for the sake of justice* [Mt 5:10].

3. Take heart and be strong [Dn 10:19]. Love God with all your heart and all your soul and all your mind, and love your neighbor as yourself. In these two commands is all the law and the prophets [Mt 22:37–40].[6] St. Augustine says: Love and do whatsoever you wish.[7]

4. Do not regret too much that you are bound to an infidel husband. Remember the holy woman Esther, who was married to the infidel prince Ahasuerus, and greatly benefited God's people.[8] And the Apostle says that an unbelieving husband will be saved through a faithful wife [1 Cor 7:14]. You are married and cannot be separated by law. You do not have witnesses willing to testify for you. You cannot otherwise be separated by ecclesiastical judgment.[9] Your desire would be to leave the world, to renounce yourself, and naked to follow the naked Christ on the cross.[10] But pray to your Lord

God that His will, not yours, be done concerning you. We read in the Gospel that the Son of God, soon to be sacrificed for us, before His Passion prayed to the Father and said, "Father, if it can be done, *let this cup pass away from me—nevertheless not as I wish, but as you will*" [Mt 26:39].

5. You should not be too anxious about changes of place and appearance. Keep God in your heart whether you are in the city, in the court, in an ivory bed, in splendid dress, whether amongst the army, sitting in judgment, or feasting. Love, and God will be with you. You stay among barbaric and rude men; it seems to you that you can do no good there. There you find simoniacal clergy, bishops and abbots and priests; wicked and thieving princes; adulterers and the incestuous—people ignorant of God's law. Nobody does good, nobody speaks good, everyone contradicts the truth. There is no truth, no mercy, no knowledge in that land. Falsehood, adultery, and murder have overflowed and bloodshed follows bloodshed [Hos 4:1–2]. *The land was polluted with blood and defiled with their works and the people steeped themselves in debauchery of their own invention. And the Lord was roused to wrath against His people and detested His own inheritance and handed them over to the heathen*—that is, those of unclean spirit[11]— *and those who hated them were masters over them* [Ps 105/106:38–41].

6. Fear not such enemies of Christ. They will not harm you in any way unless God allows it. If they hate you, curse you, and reproach you, you will be blessed. As the Gospel says: Blessed will you be when men, speaking falsely because of me, will hate you, curse you, and reproach you, and ban your name as wicked. Rejoice and exult, because your reward is abundant in heaven [Lk 5:22–23]. And again: *If the world hates you, know that it hated me first.* If you were of this world, the world would love what belonged to it, but because you are not of the world, the world hates you [Jn 15:18–19]. And in the same place:[12] *If they have called the master Beelzebub, how much more so shall they call his servants* [Mt 10:25]? And in another place: *And you will be hated by all men for my name's sake, and no hair from your head will be harmed. In your patience you possess your souls* [Lk 21:17–19]. True pa-

tience is that conquered by no rage, overcome by no tribulation. *Many are the tribulations of the righteous, and the Lord will free them from every one. The Lord stands by those whose hearts are troubled, and He will save the humble in spirit* [Ps 33/34:20,19]. And elsewhere: *I have called on the Lord in my tribulation, and the Lord in his greatness heard me. The Lord is my help; I will not fear what any man do to me. The Lord is my help, and I will scorn my enemies. It is better to trust in God than in man. It is better to have hope in God than in princes* [Ps 117/118:5–9]. And in another place: *Trust not in princes nor the sons of men, in whom there is no salvation* [Ps 145/146:2–3], *because man's salvation is in vain* [Ps 59/60:13]. And likewise: *Call upon me in your day of tribulation; I will rescue you and you will honor me* [Ps 49/50:15]. Also: *You will tear me away from the quarrels of the crowd, and you will place me at the head of nations* [Ps 17/18:44]. And in the same place: *I found tribulation and sorrow, and I called upon the name of the Lord* [Ps 114–115/116:3–4]. Likewise: *I cried out to the Lord when I was afflicted, and He heard* [Ps 119/120:1]. In another place: *Tribulation and anguish found me, but Your commandments are my meditation* [Ps 118/119:143].

7. *Hear, daughter* [Ps 44/45:11], and turn to the Scripture which says: *My help is from God who made heaven and earth* [Ps 120/121:2]. *Fear God and keep His commandments; that is everything man can do* [Eccl 12:13]. *Those who fear God want for nothing* [Ps 33/34:10].[13] All human life is temptation on earth, and the present life misery for those who know God. *All flesh is grass, and all its glory the field of grass* [Is 40:6; 1 Pt 1:24]. In whatever splendid garments it is clothed, flesh will always be flesh.[14] Thus it is written: *Vanity of vanities, all is vanity.* And whatever is under the sun is vanity and affliction of the spirit [Eccl 1:2, 14].

8. Therefore, sister, do not be puffed up by good fortune or shattered by adversity. Hold to the right path. Narrow indeed and difficult is the path which leads to life, and few walk upon it [Mt 7:14] but *whatever happens to the righteous man will not sadden him* [Prv 12:21]. Hear the Lord speaking to his friends: *You will lament and weep, but the world will rejoice. You will be sad, but your sadness will be turned to joy* [Jn 16:20]. It is necessary to enter the kingdom of heaven

through your tribulations [Acts 14:21], from the first righteous man, Abel, to the present day. For it is written: God whips *every son he receives* [Heb 12:6] and: *Blessed is the man chastened by God* [Jb 5:17]. And in Revelation: *Those whom I love I rebuke and correct* [Rv 3:19]. The Lord saved Noah in the flood. He watched over Abraham in his travels. He protected Isaac among the Philistines. He made Jacob wealthy in Mesopotamia. Joseph, sold into slavery, He raised up in Egypt. He made Moses cross over the Red Sea and He made Joshua the victor in the Promised Land and He saved faithful David from Saul's persecution. And Lot among the Sodomites remained righteous to see and hear. And He kept three boys unharmed in the fire of Babylon. He saved Daniel in the lion's den.[15] He has spiritually freed all his faithful prophets and apostles and every just person from eternal damnation.

9. Believe, love, hope in God and do good; settle in the land of your heart and *feed on its riches. Take delight in the Lord, and he will give you your heart's desire* [Ps 36/37:3–4]. Rejoice in tribulations because *tribulation gives rise to patience, patience to testing, testing to hope. Hope does not confound, because the love of God is poured out in our hearts through the Holy Spirit that has been given to us* [Rom 5:3–5].

10. You live for the time being amongst savage men; flee their wicked works in your heart. Lift up your heart to your God,[16] and let your conversation always be in heaven [Phil 3:20]. Take care lest you do good works for the praise of humankind, thereby losing God's reward [Mt 6:1–2]. In the Gospel it is written: *When you give alms, do not let your left hand know what your right hand is doing* [Mt 6:3]. That is: when you do good, which is what is meant by "your right hand," you should not do it for the praise of men, which is what is meant by "your left hand." And in the same place: *When you pray, go into your room, and pray to your Father with the door shut. And your Father, who sees all that is done in secret, will reward you* [Mt 6:6]. And again: *When you fast, do not be gloomy, like the hypocrites* [Mt 6:16].

11. To give alms and pray and fast: these are good works if they are done for God, but profit nothing if done for the praise of

mankind. Short prayer is beneficial. Prayer from the heart, not the lips, is acceptable to God. God does not pay heed to words, but to the heart of the one who prays. All good works of the just are prayer. We can always pray in our hearts, but not always with our mouths. It is written in the Gospel: Do not prattle in prayer, like heathens who think they will be heard in their loquacity [Mt 6:7]. But pray to the Father: *Our Father, who art in heaven* [Mt 6:9].[17] Keep this Lord's prayer in your heart, from memory, always. When you are occupied with much business, make short prayers. In the morning hear the canonical hours properly: Matins, Prime, Terce, Sext, None, and later Vespers and Compline. Hear the hours of the blessed Virgin Mary every day.[18]

12. Many clerics are hypocrites. Monks and hermits, in order to please men, pretend to make long prayers that they might be seen by men.[19] But you, far removed from all vanity and pretense: hold to the truth discreetly. It is written of the Lord Jesus Christ that He stayed awake all night praying in the mountains [Lk 6:12] and performed miracles by day in the cities. To pray at night with God in the mountain means to love God with the heart's desire. To work miracles by day with God in the city means to live for the good of those around you. Love voluntary poverty. Amidst positions and honors, amidst riches and silk garments, amidst husband and beloved children and splendid parents, sighing along with the prophet say: I am a needy woman and poor, and the Lord watches over me [Ps 39/40:18].[20]

13. Concerning your sin of incest and the sin of your daughter whom you have given over to death: anxious and troubled, humbly and submissively, pray to God that he free you, lest you perish. You cannot be separated from your husband by ecclesiastical law. You have done what you could: you fled. The Church brought you back. For your daughter, seek separation by any means available. Otherwise, carry forever grief in your heart for so despicable a deed.[21]

14. Do not disclose your will and your plan to all your house-

hold and friends. Many are your friends for their own advantage, but few are faithful friends and advisors for the sake of God and your soul. Arrange nothing and do nothing casually. Do everything deliberately, lest you regret it later. Be merciful to all the poor, but still more toward the destitute and *most of all to the servants of faith* [Gal 6:10], those who have left the world for God.[22] Hear the Lord saying: *Blessed are the merciful, for they shall obtain mercy* [Mt 5:7]. And again: *Be merciful just as your Father is merciful* [Lk 6:36], *who makes His sun rise above the good and the wicked, and makes it rain on the just and the unjust* [Mt 5:45]. And elsewhere Scripture says: *He apportioned and gave to the poor, and His justice abides forever* [Ps 111/112:9]. It did not say he gave to the rich, but to the poor. Alms free man from death and do not allow him to go into darkness [Tb 4:11] if they were acquired rightly. But if they were ill-gotten, they do not help but harm, as the Scripture makes plain: He who makes an offering from the pillage of the poor is like one who sacrifices a son in the sight of his father [Sir 34:24].

15. Exercise caution and discretion in all things—in abstinence, in fasting, in vigils, in prayers. Eat and drink and sleep in such measure that you can endure toil for the sake of others, not yourself. I do not tell you to nourish the flesh, because whoever nourishes the flesh nourishes the Enemy. But I do tell you not to kill the flesh immoderately, because he who kills the flesh kills its inhabitant.[23] The first man was seduced not by delectable foods, but by the fruit of a tree. Esau lost his birthright for a meal of beans, not chicken. Elijah ate meat, and was taken up to heaven. Christ ate fish, and drank wine.[24] The kingdom of God is not food and drink, but grace and peace [Rom 14:17]. Amen.

2. Charters

"Charter" *(carta, charta)* was the general medieval term for any written document. The Magna Carta (Great Charter) issued by King John of England in 1215 is the most famous example. Since for much of the Middle Ages literacy was the preserve of the religious elite, charters commonly memorialize agreements between parties, at least one of which was often a religious person or institution. Property was the central concern of many charters, as they recorded the donation, sale, exchange, or other arrangements concerning land or money. Medieval charters served primarily as records of events, the meetings of parties involved in a given transaction or accord. Written documentation was becoming much more common in Europe during Robert of Arbrissel's lifetime, because an increasingly populous, vital, and complex society found it useful to have a reminder of past events. To us, this is obvious, but for many centuries there had been far greater reliance on oral agreements and human memory. The expansion of the written record had enormous implications for how European society operated and, for historians, how much about it can be discovered. Largely owing to the new habit of writing things down, we are much better informed about European history since the eleventh century than for most of the half-millennium before 1000 A.D.

In the charters translated below, Robert of Arbrissel describes two agreements. The first is between Robert and his patron Bishop Peter II of Poitiers. Robert places Fontevraud, its daughter houses, and its other properties in the diocese of Poitiers under the bishop's protection, offering in exchange the prayers of the nuns of Fontevraud in his lifetime and thereafter, plus an annual tribute to the treasury of the diocese. The pact was made less than a decade after the foundation of Fontevraud, but apparently the diverse community described by Baudri of Dol had already become less eclectic: Robert refers to Fontevraud simply as a church of nuns and promises specifically that it is the nuns who will pray for Bishop Peter, whose guidance and help he gratefully acknowledges. The existence of such an agreement also shows that Robert was unwilling to take full responsibility for the religious congregation he had founded, intent as he was on continuing his mission of errant evangelism and pursuit of ascetic religious devotion.

The second charter Robert addressed to Gerald of Sales (ca. 1070–1120), a companion from Robert's days as a hermit in the forest of Craon. He was the founder of numerous religious houses in southwestern France. The present document records Robert's donation to Gerald of two estates originally obtained for Robert and the nuns of Fontevraud. It shows that Robert remained in contact with an old friend, for he had left eremitical life for full-time preaching nearly twenty years earlier. It also demonstrates that Robert was not determined to found priories of Fontevraud everywhere. He visited the bishop and cathedral canons of the city of Périgueux who, impressed with his preaching, granted him some property belonging to the diocese for the benefit of the nuns of Fontevraud. Other local lords made donations of land, too, but Robert decided not to retain these properties, instead giving them to Gerald with the permission of Abbess Petronilla and the nuns of Fontevraud. Afterward, the bishop, the canons, and the local lay patrons ratified Robert's donation to Gerald. These properties were the first patrimony of what became the monastery of Cadouin, which in 1119 joined the Cistercian Order, known for its strict adherence to the Rule of St. Benedict and the austerity of its monks. The monks of Cadouin established several other houses. It was thus the head of a second monastic federation established through Robert's efforts, albeit one with a history and character very different from Fontevraud.

TEXTS: PL 162: 1085–1088 (A) and *Le cartulaire de l'abbaye de Cadouin,* edited by J.-M. Maubourguet (Cahors, 1926), 9–11 (B)

A. To Bishop Peter of Poitiers (1109)

To Peter, by the grace of God venerable bishop of Poitiers, and to the venerable canons of the Holy Mother Church of Poitiers and to their successors, Brother Robert of Arbrissel offers his greetings and due obedience.

The monastery of nuns that we have founded in honor of the

Holy Mother of God and ever virgin Mary, aided by the mercy of her Son and, reverend Father Peter, by your astute participation, in your diocese at the place called Fontevraud—that church we entrust and commend in perpetuity to your patronage and care, second only to the Lord's. We do this in order that Fontevraud, like an obedient daughter, be specially joined to your Church in a charter of love, as to a very dear mother, and so that the thorns of Enemy assaults may be cut away from this new transplant by the scythe of your protection and so that she may bear fruit in the harvest of holy religious life [2 Cor 9:10]. Our Lord Jesus Christ has gathered together many nuns through me, a priest although unworthy,[25] in the abovementioned place and He has called them away from luxurious living to the honor and glory of His name. Having forgotten their worldly cares under the shield of your protection, reverend Father, may they tame the flesh, strengthen the spirit, and be ever intent on divine service just as at the beginning.[26]

To that same protection we deliver all the places in your diocese, houses of men and of nuns, belonging to the monastery of Fontevraud—that is, the houses of nuns at La Puye between Chauvigny and Angles-sur-l'Anglin, and the properties at Lencloître and Guesnes, and any other places they possess or will in the future possess justly and canonically.[27] We make this surrender and commendation of the monastery of Fontevraud to your protection, most beloved brothers, in accordance with the collective resolve of the sisters of that same church; you receive it in accordance with the resolve of your dearest Father, the venerable Bishop Peter, and all of your clergy. In exchange for such a true favor of protection, the handmaids of Christ who are or will be at Fontevraud will do two things: pray for you daily while you live, and when one of you dies, render the same service to the Lord for the soul of the deceased brother as they would do for the soul of a nun of their own congregation who had left this world. And in memory of such charity let there be an annual tribute from Fontevraud to the Church of Poitiers in the amount of 12 silver pennies, to be paid at the Pentecost synod.[28] May the omnipotent God preserve your fellowship in religious life, dearest brothers.

The mark of Bishop Peter, the mark of Dean Aimeric, the mark of Cantor Geoffrey, the mark of Archdeacon William, the mark of Archdean Hervé, the mark of Treasurer Rainer, the mark of Schoolmaster William, the mark of all the canons, the mark of Robert of Arbrissel, the mark of the nun Hersende, the mark of Petronilla, the mark of all the nuns of Fontevraud.[29]

Pronounced in synod at Poitiers in the year of the Incarnation of the Lord 1109, the second indiction, seventeenth epact, thirteen kalends of July,[30] in the reigns of Pope Pascal II; Peter, bishop of the Church of the Poitevins; Louis, king of the Franks; and William, duke of the Aquitainians. Done happily in Christ Jesus, amen.

B. To Gerald of Sales (1115)

I, Robert of Arbrissel, grant and confer irrevocably, on no terms other than the perpetuation of love in charitable brother-hood,[31] to lord Gerald of Sales, venerable master, most kind companion in times of necessity, and to his sons and fellow servants, both present and future, two properties in the forest of Cadouin. These are in Val-Seguin, which Gerald himself along with his comrades had acquired as if for himself in my person, and which acquisition he built, and also in the place named La Salvetat.[32] I relinquish as well anything whatsoever granted to me (or to another in my stead) in the aforementioned forest. And I leave these properties to their control and good will, so that they may fight for God there under the rule of lordly vassalage.[33] I decree that this grant, genuine and solemnly effected before the nuns' general chapter—with the assent and permission of Petronilla, their most faithful mother, the handmaid of the handmaids of God[34]—that it remain undisturbed and inviolable, and henceforth I ban entirely, eradicate, and completely forbid any claims dispute or contention.

The grant of the aforementioned places was made at Fontevraud on the feast of the blessed Benedict, the fifth ides of July in the year of the Incarnation of the Lord 1115,[35] in the sixteenth year of the reign of Pope Pascal, in the eighth indiction, during vacancy in the see of Poitiers, Bishop Peter having gone the way of all flesh and in the reigns of Louis, king of the Franks, and William, duke of the Aquitainians.

They bear witness to such things who are so entitled: Fulk, consul[36] of the Angevins; Pagan of Clairvaux; Archiliosus; Simon Enfandi; Aimeric, son of Arbert the viscount of Thouars; Bartholomew Lopez; Bernard of Saponar, clerk; Pagan, priest; Warren of Troy; Rainald of Subnonea; Aimeric the Cheese; and Pagan the Teacher, son of viscount Arbert above.[37]

3. Statutes for Fontevraud (ca. 1115)

From its origins as a loosely organized assortment of heterogeneous religious seekers, Fontevraud quickly developed into a fairly traditional medieval monastic community—the significant difference being that sisters and brothers lived and worshiped together at Fontevraud and her burgeoning daughter houses. The women were guided by the Rule of St. Benedict. But Robert does not refer to the male element of his community as monks or canons, so their status and daily life apparently did not conform to either the Benedictine Rule or the Rule of St. Augustine, which the canons of La Roë followed (see Baudri's *vita*, sections 12 and 15). They are instead *fratres*, brothers. One of Robert's key concerns at the end of his life was the functioning of this unusual community of religious women and men.

According to Andreas's *vita*, section 10, at the time he appointed Petronilla abbess of Fontevraud, Robert issued a series of commands about speech, action, food, and clothing at the abbey. Three rules of Fontevraud have survived but no single one contains discussion of all four matters. Nor do they contain Robert's command that no cloister nun should ever be made abbess (as reported by Andreas) or any evidence for the claim made by Pope Innocent II in a letter of 1132 that Robert had specifically forbidden the nuns to use violent means to protect their property. However, exacting textual analysis of the three texts led the German scholar Johannes von Walter to conclude that one of them is a fragment of the original and dates to ca. 1115. That fragment is translated here. Some of it is probably very close to or even identical to what Robert wrote or dictated in late 1115; a few stipulations are clearly those of Petronilla, as usual concerned with her authority over the brothers and the practical operations of what had become a wealthy religious corporation with a constellation of affiliated institutions.

These precepts demand a strict life for both men and women. For the nuns, Robert stressed silence, a traditional monastic virtue, and even forbade the use of sign language common in monasteries. He also prohibited all eating of meat, a more austere measure than in the Rule of St. Benedict—and one that disappears from collections of precepts written down after his death—and is careful to prevent contact of men and women that might be occasion for sin or even gossip. As in the deliberations reported by Andreas, Robert's primary dictate to the brothers is that they remain in the service of, and obedient to, the women of Fontevraud. More about Robert's notions of the spirituality of male and female cooperation is suggested by the two letters to him translated below.

TEXT: PL 162: 1083–1085

Among the oldest statutes given to Petronilla, first abbess, and the nuns of the church of Fontevraud by the most reverend father Master Robert, for the purpose of perpetuating religious life and discipline, are these:

1. Cloister nuns are to keep silence at all times, except those who manage external business.[38]

2. They are to make no gestures or signs unless they are necessary.[39]

3. They are never to eat flesh or blood food, even when ill.[40]

4. Ailing sisters are not to be anointed or take communion except in church.[41]

5. Petronilla, chosen by Master Robert and made abbess by the common will and pious request of both the nuns and the religious brothers, is to have and hold the power to rule the monastery of Fontevraud and all places belonging to it, and they should obey her. They are to revere her as their spiritual mother, and all business of the church, spiritual and secular, is to remain under her wise care, or she may delegate to whomever she likes and as she decides.[42]

6. The abbess herself, looking to the future, decreed the following: the major prioress is to be received everywhere, and both at Fontevraud and in all her daughter houses they are to obey her, and she is to have power second to the abbess in transacting business for the monastery.

7. When the abbess dies, the prioress is to hold her position and have full power of ruling the monastery until another abbess is chosen in her place.[43]

He [Robert] gave devout precepts as follows to the priests, clerics, and laymen who had received the habit of holy life through his teaching. They promised of their own voluntary good will and pure love that they would serve the nuns under the bonds of obedience unto death: it is the reverence of due submission. They will perform this submission not only at Fontevraud but in all the daughter houses under its authority.

1. They are to celebrate the canonical divine office.[44]

2. They are to keep claustral and communal life without personal possessions, satisfied with those things that are granted them by the nuns.[45]

3. They are to be bled three times a year.[46]

4. Leftovers from the brothers' meals are to be taken to the nuns' gate and given to the poor there.[47]

5. They are not to receive as gifts parish churches or their tithes.[48]

6. They are not to lend their possessions to secular persons.

7. No stranger is to be received in the brothers' community without the permission of the abbess.

MARBODE OF RENNES, LETTER TO ROBERT OF ARBRISSEL (CA. 1098)

Marbode, cathedral schoolmaster, writer, and finally bishop of Rennes in Brittany, was born in or near Angers around 1035. He attended the local school affiliated with the bishop's church of Saint-Maurice in Angers. His teacher was Rainald, who had been trained by Fulbert of Chartres (ca. 970–1028), the first great figure in the Loire Valley's intellectual revival to which Marbode subsequently made a significant contribution. Marbode became a teacher in the Angers cathedral school and then, in the late 1070s, succeeded Rainald as its director. His famous pupils included Abbot Geoffrey of Vendôme, whose own letter to Robert of Arbrissel is translated below, and his circle of literary companions included Baudri of Dol, who wrote the first biography of Robert. Marbode was eventually named archdeacon of the diocese of Angers, the second-highest office after bishop, and was elected bishop of Rennes in 1096. He served that diocese for more than twenty-five years, returning to his native Angers at a very advanced age to die, in September 1123, at the monastery of Saint-Aubin. The monks of Saint-Aubin wrote a notice of his death in which they described Marbode as "eloquent in speech, outstanding in religion, renowned for moral integrity, and extremely accomplished in literature." They also noted that his eloquence was sweeter than honey, but his words flavored with salt—a sharp and even biting wit evident in his writings.

Marbode's literary output was prodigious. His verse includes retellings of biblical stories like that of Ruth, rhyming metric saints' lives, lyric on sacred and profane subjects, verse epistles to noblewomen including the same Countess Ermengarde of Brittany to whom Robert of Arbrissel's *Sermo* is addressed, and a *Book of Stones* describing the medical and magical properties of some minerals. Most admired of all is a mature work, the *Book of Ten Chapters*, ten long poems on subjects including the proper approach to writing, the characteristics of good and evil women, and the joys and pains of old age.

Marbode wrote less prose, or at least less of it has survived: a few *vitae* and six letters, one to Robert of Arbrissel. Robert had spent some time in Angers in the 1090s and knew Marbode there, leaving for his stint as a hermit-a few years before Marbode was elected bishop. It is not hard to imagine a strong clash of personalities and interests between the sophisticated and acerbic poet-ecclesiastic and the restless ascetic who had fled church office in the diocese of Rennes. After Robert left his canons at La Roë for good, but before he founded Fontevraud, the bishop (as he had become) wrote the letter translated below.

Letters in the classical and medieval worlds were neither strictly private communications nor public writings as we would understand them. Before the twelfth century, letters were prized more for eloquence and rhetorical flourish than for intimacy or inventiveness. The *ars dictamen*, the art of epistolary composition, was a branch of rhetoric taught in schools like the one Marbode headed. In Marbode's time, the *ars dictamen* itself became the subject of learned treatises and textbooks. The eleventh and twelfth centuries saw the zenith of medieval epistolography, as writers became more learned and communications became more regular and extensive. Only implicitly, however, do Marbode's letters share in his age's trend toward more personal and self-conscious writing. The most famous and passionate correspondence of this type was between the theologian Abelard (1079–1142) and his one-time student and lover Heloise (ca. 1101–1163). That intense exchange dates to only a few decades after this letter to Robert of Arbrissel, but despite the self-revelatory nature of some of Marbode's poetry, the bishop made Robert and his detractors the focus.

Marbode follows the traditional format of letter writing, including five standard parts: salutation, introduction, narration, petition, and conclusion. He writes as a bishop to rebuke one of his spiritual sons. His complaints in the narration fall under four headings, all linked to the theme announced in his opening sentences of salutation and introduction: appropriate action and the consequences of careless or inappropriate behavior. Nearly a third of the letter laments that Robert's relations with women give rise to rumor and scandal. The bishop lays out a scorching critique of women as sexual temptresses and bemoans the folly of Robert's choice to gather men and women together in his fellowship. Next, Robert's personal appearance comes in for criticism as both ludicrous and self-aggrandizing. The third section of the narration describes a demagogue, a preacher who slanders churchmen, whose charisma draws attention and support away from local clergy, and who indiscriminately thrusts the young, ignorant, and inexperienced into religious service whose only rule is admiration of their master. After a harsh description of the fate of some young women in Robert's sway, Marbode sums up briefly with his fourth charge, which gathers together the first three: Robert has betrayed his obligations to stability and order by shirking responsibility for the community of men he left at La Roë in favor of his female followers.

As befits a bishop who also wrote a treatise on rhetorical ornamentation, Marbode chooses his words carefully. He never directly accuses Robert of any malfeasance, instead expressing his complaints in terms of what is said or reported. Thus the letter is in one sense no more than a collection of unpleasant rumors, but through several tricks, among them by attributing the stories to humble and mighty alike, and by repeatedly invoking common sense and reason in his critique, Marbode makes his brief perhaps even more shocking by portraying it as the fair accusation of an array of observers. Marbode manages to be harsh without turning his letter into a personal attack. Before he begins the litany of complaints and again at the very end of the letter, Marbode urges Robert to respond to the charges reasonably (the petition of the epistolary tradition) or else, he concludes, the preacher must fear hell.

Several questions arise from Marbode's letter. The most obvious is how much of it we should take literally. Were there really a number of naive girls who joined Robert's followers, got pregnant, and left their newfound spiritual family in disgrace? Did Robert actually look quite as bizarre as Marbode says, and encourage his followers to the same radical nonconformity of dress and behavior?

Related to the accuracy of Marbode's portrayal is the question of his motives. When he wrote, Marbode was a newly elected bishop who had earlier written poetry on sexual subjects, for example, a twelve-line lyric concerning a youth's lewd behavior with another male. Was Marbode trying to deflect criticism of his suitability for the position of bishop? Was he perhaps trying to get Robert to refrain from doing things he might later regret? Or was he simply acting as a prelate, upset by reports that Robert's actions in the name of religion had disastrous consequences for some of the preacher's followers and for the parish priests whom Marbode supervised as archdeacon and bishop?

Finally, it is difficult to assess Marbode's opinion of women, in this letter and other writings. Here he focuses on female bodies as sites of danger and pollution, as he did in one of the sections of the *Book of Ten Chapters*. But he also wrote a companion poem full of classical and biblical examples of female virtues and wrote playful and respectful verse letters to women. In any case, Marbode's accusations should be compared with other accounts of Robert, both critical and laudatory, and considered in the context of the author's other writings and new responsibilities as bishop.

TEXT: Marbode of Rennes, *Incipit liber Marbodi . . .* , edited by Yves Mayeuc (Rennes, 1524), 76–79. The modern edition by Johannes von Walter, *Die ersten*

Wanderprediger Frankreichs: Studien zur Geschichte des Mönchtums, 2 volumes (Leipzig, 1903–1906) 1: 181–189 is far better than the version in PL 171: 1480–1486.

1. The least of bishops to God's servant Robert—not only to offer righteously, but also to apportion righteously.[1] As often as I hear about your brotherhood—that it adorns the Christian faith and that its imitation by your followers can redound to your credit—not only do I rejoice for your sake but also I give joyful thanks to our leader Christ, whose sweet fragrance is spread far and wide by you through His gift [2 Cor 2:14–15]. However, when certain things are alleged to be said and done by you, things contrary to sound doctrine and honorable life, I am troubled by sadness and fear, lest the crafty Enemy plants some evil seed amidst your good crops, God forbid, or you yourself arrange good works with naive and indiscriminate carelessness. 2. In building walls there must be reasoned consideration not just of the materials, but also of the suitability of design. Otherwise things good in themselves begin, if badly done, to displease. In the same way a skilled speaker pays attention not only to what sort of words he uses, but how and when and to whom.

3. For it is fitting to your profession, dear friend—you who have turned the eyes of all toward yourself by the novel eccentricity of your appearance and deportment and have put forth in yourself an example over and beyond the cloak and sandals of the strongest philosophy—it is fitting that you exhibit nothing in words or deeds that can be found contrary to sacred authorities or that would offend those who might otherwise have been edified.[2] For the Apostle says *Give no offense to Jews or gentiles or the Church of God* [1 Cor 10:32] and elsewhere *Do not let our good be called evil* [Rom 14:16]. Therefore give careful scrutiny to your life and your talk so that you provide the Enemy no occasion to hurl curses. 4. You ought to remember the heavenly creatures, described as all eyes in front and behind, in whose numbers you are reckoned.[3] Carrying the good news of Christ, you have mounted Aminadab's chariot.[4] So see to it, my very beloved son, that in relying too much in your own holi-

ness you do not become a stumbling block or a trap for weaker members and thereby a weak brother, for whom Christ died, perish on your conscience. So if you sin, says the Apostle, *striking their weak consciences, you sin against Christ* [1 Cor 8:12].

5. But lest I seem to go on in generalities and do not so much rebuke you for noteworthy actions as note what ought to be rebuked, I shall indicate specifically the things that entice into sin the most people in your company. Thus if you recognize fault, you will not fail to make correction; if otherwise, you may refute the error of unfavorable opinion with reasonable explanation.

You are said to love greatly cohabitation with women—in which matter you once sinned[5]—in order that you may strive to purify the contamination of old wickedness, purportedly in the name of new religious practice, using the same material.[6] 6. You deign to join women not only by day at a common table but also by night in a common bed—or so it is reported. Your whole flock of disciples does likewise so that you, lying in the middle amongst them, obstruct the laws of wakefulness and sleep for both sexes.[7] They say that women follow you on your wanderings and are constantly by your side when you preach. 7. They assert also that you keep not a small number of women in different places and regions, in hospices and lodgings,[8] women intermingled with men (not with impunity), on the pretext that you have assigned them to the care of the poor and pilgrims. How dangerous is this practice the wailing of babies, to not put too fine a point on it, has betrayed.

8. On this count, therefore, most people reproach your way of life, not only ecclesiastics but common folk too, since surely divine and human laws loudly protest this kind of association. The beginning of sin was caused by a woman and through her we all die, so if we want to avoid sin, we must cut the cause of sin away from us.[9] As Scripture attests, he who loves danger falls into danger [Sir 3:27]. 9. You, casting your nets widely, catch a great quantity of fish, but some say that among the fish you also draw snakes, which cannot easily change their deadly nature. You cannot handle snakes

safely: the sight of them cannot but be harmful since seeing them breeds not fear but concupiscence. About them divine Scripture says that asps hiss disease and woman spreads the plague of lust.[10] Solomon makes the following comparison: *Moths come out from clothing and the wickedness of man from woman* [Sir 42:13], whence it says elsewhere *But woman snatches man's precious soul* [Prv 6:26].[11]

10. Take care, accordingly, that your catch does not catch you.[12] It is not safe to sleep long with a serpent nearby. But if you respond that you are wakeful, and keep vigilant guard for your whole watch—well, such serpents are accustomed to inflict wounds even on the vigilant. Indeed with one look they pour caressing poison into the marrow and tempt the recesses of the mind with insatiable lust. Remove yourself, I beg you, from temptations of this sort, which even if they do not harm your soul with your consent, doubtless stain your reputation and give religion a bad name.

11. How great a sin this is Augustine shows in his book on the celibacy of the clergy, saying, "To keep culpable continence and bring chastity into disrepute is worse than fornication."[13] But how can we know whether or not this close association is not harming you? As Jerome says, "He whose face you look on constantly ministers to you perilously." Also: "You should not rely on your former chastity, because you cannot be holier than David, nor wiser than Solomon," both of whom we know came to grief through a woman.[14] 12. Even if you do not fornicate bodily, without a doubt you cannot stay chaste in soul for long while living among women. For you are not of that passionless kindred of eunuchs, who are born that way and therefore have no reward for it; rather you strive to be one of those who make themselves eunuchs for the kingdom of heaven, of whom it is said: I will give them a place of renown in my house and within my walls, a renown better than sons and daughters [Is 56:5]. These men struggle, for without great effort they can scarcely master illicit carnal appetites even in the absence of women.[15] What if the fire nears the chaff?[16] It will undoubtedly ignite a poisonous flame, or surely increase the difficulty of the struggle.

13. As Augustine confirms, moreover, it is quite absurd to think that "anyone given the opportunity to triumph in luxury would want to be constrained to labor."[17] For if "someone puts himself forward and says 'What I want I shall win' it is the same as 'I desire to live under threat of destruction.'" But why should we hesitate to add a certain detail from Augustine's text, on the basis of which alone the whole heart of guilty cohabitation may be laid bare? "So why," he asks, "does anyone who disdains marriage devote attention to a woman? Someone who does not eat meat—why does he fill his house with preparations for meat? And if he doesn't drink wine, why does he enjoy the pleasure of wine? As if in always having it and not tasting it, the eater's soul is not nourished with delicacies, nor his desire often aroused by the smell of wine alone! Why does he wish, through hypocrisy, to be called abstinent by his fellow men and swell up with meat and wine in secret? Many people have riches of which they deny themselves the use, but grasp greedily; if greed had not taken hold of them, they would not possess its distinguishing marks. But because they are possessed by greed, they enjoy in their heart of hearts that of which they make no practical use. 14. So likewise he who disdains the bonds of marriage yet is bound otherwise by feminine chains (even though there be no sex) is always tied by desire, sight, conversation, intimacy. If he had no desire for women, he would never consider a woman among his pleasures. Indeed he makes a claim that seems suspect, this man who has taken an unlawful wife and foregone a lawful one. Unless I am mistaken, it has been proven that men vow chastity in public yet are not without wives in private. The two proofs of chastity and lust, for and against, are to be marveled at." And Augustine added much else in this vein, which shows clearly the dishonorable intent of this sort of relationship. We think this can suffice regarding the first count.

15. Furthermore, many think you ought to be reproached for the extreme strangeness of your ragged clothes—and quite rightly, since it seems appropriate neither to the profession of canon in which you started your service nor the priestly order to which you

were promoted. For each and every order and profession there is a fitting and proper dress code, which if violated offends public opinion. "A wise man will not upset public standards, nor turn people to himself by novelty."[18] Indeed we ought to do just as Seneca says. It is fitting to appropriate moral judgments of pagan philosophers just as gold and silver vessels were taken from the Egyptians [Ex 12:35–36]. We must therefore behave so as to follow a life better than the common one, not contrary to it. Otherwise those whom we desire to correct we put to flight and turn away from us. Philosophy promises this first of all: difference will not exempt any profession from common sense, humanity, and fellowship. 16. Let us see to it that those things by which we want to procure admiration do not become ridiculous and reviled. Thus reason is to be observed and moderation preserved in the mean and humble guise of common sense and with the authority of custom. It is one thing to go about decked out in finery, another to wear clean clothes: the former seems to pertain to vanity, the latter to virtue. Likewise it is a long way from cheap and ordinary clothing to coarse tatters. The first befits religion and modesty, the latter shows instead stupidity and a careless spirit.

17. Just as it is a sign of dissipation to desire finery, it is a sign of madness to shun what is ordinary and inexpensive to obtain. The toga should not dazzle, but nor should it become filthy. It is far more praiseworthy to be humble in silk than to glory in rags. As Jerome says to Nepotian: "Avoid drab grey dress as much as dazzling white. Both pretentious and tattered clothes should be equally avoided, since the one smacks of pleasure, the other of pride. What is praiseworthy is not going around without linen clothing, but rather not having the money to buy it."[19]

18. They say that you go into the crowd, having discarded your canonical dress, skin covered by a hairshirt and a worn-out cowl full of holes, your legs half-naked, your beard long and your hair trimmed at the brow, barefoot, offering a strange spectacle to all who look on such that you lack only a club to complete the outfit

of a lunatic. 19. All this procures for you not so much a moral authority among the "simple folk," as you are wont to say, as the suspicion of madness among the wise. . . .[20] Therefore, I beg you: return to common sense, and do not strive for holiness alone and without precedent, since the wise man says: *Woe to the lone man, because if he falls there is no one to help him up* [Eccl 4:10]. The prophet, too, urges us not to devise novelties, but rather to follow in the footsteps of the ancients: *Stand by the wayside and look and ask which of the venerable paths is the good way and walk in it and you will find your soul's delight* [Jer 6:16]. 20. If you fancy yourself to be following in the path of John the Baptist, very well: first fulfill the measure of the confessors and apostles, so that you may thereby ascend to him, who has never had equal of woman born.[21] Reason dictates that just as there is no fall from the depths, there is no starting from the heights.

21. Next: in those sermons you customarily teach crowds of common and ignorant people, you censure not only the vices of those present—as is fitting—but also those of absent churchmen. You enumerate the crimes not only of those in orders but even in high offices—which is not fitting—and you slander and abuse. It seems to me that this is to mingle poison with its antidote, or that out of the same hole, against the order of nature, salt water and fresh flow, as the holy apostle James says.[22] 22. This is to disparage, not to preach. Moreover I fail to see what purpose there can be in condemnation of absent persons or what spiritual gain might come of it; it seems to give license for unlettered listeners to sin when you place before them as bad examples their betters, by whose authority they could protect themselves. This is the quality of superiors: whatever they do they appear to teach. The absent accused may be angry and complain at your disparagement instead of being challenged to correction by it.

23. But perhaps it profits you if, once the ecclesiastical order becomes worthless in common view, you alone with your followers are held worthy. There are some who understand the situation in

just that way. But this cunning sounds like the old man; it is earthly, animalistic, diabolical; it is not fitting to your profession, your journeying, your rags.[23] Even if you deny that you have courted this opinion, you cannot deny that you have acquired it. 24. We see impoverished priests, deserted as if unworthy by their congregations.[24] To *them* their flock should make offerings, to *their* prayers commend themselves, from *them* accept the charge of penance, pay *them* tithes and first-fruits. And all of these pastors lament that they are condemned by your unjust reproach. We see crowds flocking to you from all sides, bestowing marks of honor[25] on you and yours that they owe their own priests. What leads these people, it is clear, is not the love of religion but what is always and everywhere characteristic of the crowd: curiosity and desire for novelty. Nor do their lives appear improved. So it happens that others' losses serve your advantage.

25. Furthermore, there is also this charge to be answered in some fashion: you indiscriminately receive all sorts and conditions of men and women who, as it transpires, are pricked with conscience by your preaching, and then immediately you bind these untested people with religious vows. Mind the Apostle's words: *Test the spirits to see if they are from God* [1 Jn 4:1]. The blessed Pope Gregory, writing to Bishop Fortunatus about not rashly accepting converts to religious life says, among other things, "Since it is a serious matter for someone untried to make allegiance to men, who can say how much more serious it is to commit the untested to God's service?"[26]

26. So it happens that most people, having fallen back on their former ways, incur double damnation. Indeed you take no further responsibility for some you have failed to constrain in any regular discipline, but permit each to do his own bidding.[27] Either you are content with the invocation of your name over them, as certain people think, or you know not to lose time dealing with those already snared, since you are, as you yourself declare, avid for new gain. Word has it you say one night suffices for you to prevent sin.

27. Indeed your purpose goes on to infinity: ever neglectful of those who have come before, you take responsibility for new followers. In this way, the damnation of those neglected increases at the same rate as the number of your disciples grows. You should fear becoming one of the former, about whom the Lord said, *Woe to you, scribes and Pharisees, you hypocrites, who scour land and sea to make one convert, and when he is made, you make him a son of Hell twice over* [Mt 23:15]. If there is woe for those making one such convert, what must it be like for those who make so very many like him? For if the damnation of one condemns many, so much more will the damnation of many redound upon the one responsible.

28. The number of your converts is so great that we see them running around different lands in groups, clad in coarse garments. Identifiable by the length of their beards, they go about through the fields in shoes, it is said, but barefoot in villages and towns. If you ask them why, they reply that they are "the Master's men." They do not usually say which master, so that an unqualified answer proclaims your excellence. 29. This much is pretty clear: these are men and they walk like men [1 Cor 3:3]. But God forbid that they really have it from your teaching that they should behave and speak as the whole world knows they do. We prefer their faults be attributed to your negligence than bolstered by your authority.

30. I say nothing about the young girls whom, as I said above, professing to religious vocation without testing, dress changed to match, you have at once sequestered in numerous cells.[28] Their first attempts, even if under guardianship of a rule, would have offered much to fear. The sorry result shows the temerity of this undertaking: some have slipped away, jail breakers ready to give birth; others have had their babies in these same cells.[29] None of this would have happened if you in your wisdom had given any thought to consequences—or rather, if you carefully heeded the Lord's words in which he teaches how in imposing burdens the strength of the bearers must be measured, showing in a fitting image how greater commands are inappropriate to lesser people. No one, He said,

puts new wine in old wineskins, or the skins break and the wine spills. And no one sews an unwashed patch onto old clothes, or the new patch falls off the old and makes a larger tear [Mt 9:16–17]. 31. So it has happened to these wretched little women without much experience and divested of their old life whom you have hastily given over to the demands of new perfection. Their clothes were torn by their swelling wombs; they spurned moral teachings and the tear in their souls has been made much worse. Their wombs are burst from the spilling of childbirth, and they have lost their wineskins by scorning commandments.[30] For the old skin did not contain the new ardor for such high virtue. So your religion is held liable for this outcome, because there was no discretion, mother of all virtues, at the beginning. 32. Therefore, dearest brother, instructed by these present perils, you must apply more diligent care in these matters hereafter and especially you must offer prayers to God with supplication, so that the same God and *Lord may watch over your coming and going now and forever* [Ps 120/121:8].

33. The last count, seemingly not out of tune with the first, is your fault as regards the profession of canonical life, the stability of your prior place and your responsibility for the supervision of the brothers professed there—all of which you are said to have disregarded for the sisters' sake.[31]

34. We ask from your brotherhood a reasonable reply to this charge, or else we fear your certain damnation. On this matter there is a great deal more to be said against you, but we prefer to wait on what will be said by you. May Christ keep watch over your faith as you pray for us, dearest brother.

GEOFFREY OF VENDÔME,
LETTER TO ROBERT OF
ARBRISSEL (CA. I 107)

Geoffrey was abbot of the Benedictine monastery of La Trinité in Vendôme. The house, located northwest of Tours, was founded in 1040 by the Count Geoffrey Martel of Anjou and Countess Agnes, daughter of the duke of Aquitaine. The future abbot was born around 1070, a member of the family of the lords of Craon, a nephew of Robert of Arbrissel's patron Rainald, who helped to found La Roë, and a relation by marriage of Petronilla of Chemillé. Geoffrey studied at the cathedral school in Angers under Marbode of Rennes, where his education included the Roman classics, the Bible, the Church Fathers, and law. He entered the monastery at Vendôme and was elected, still very young, as abbot in 1093. The already wealthy and powerful abbey prospered under Geoffrey's leadership, which lasted until his death in 1132.

Abbot Geoffrey sponsored intellectual pursuits at Vendôme, but his chief concerns were pious and institutional. Nearly 200 of his letters have survived, carefully collected and copied shortly before his death. His correspondents were overwhelmingly ecclesiastical, as was his mentality. Geoffrey was deeply imbued with the spirit and letter of the Rule of St. Benedict, which gave enormous responsibilities to the abbot. Geoffrey took this charge seriously and wrote on matters both theoretical and practical. He was a tireless advocate of ecclesiastical reform and purity, writing and acting repeatedly to limit lay involvement with Church mission and property. He was a tenacious advocate of what he thought right or, more to the point, what he thought were the rights owed to himself, his monastery, and the Roman Church. He harassed some correspondents repeatedly on the same subject, cared little if he made enemies, and did not hesitate to tell popes, in particular Pascal II and Calixtus II, where their duty lay. Around 1106 he wrote to Countess Ermengarde of Brittany, commanding her to overcome temptation and persist in the choice to leave the secular world—a decision that did not last, as Robert of Arbrissel's letter to her shows. Geoffrey was an idealist with the utmost respect for what he regarded as the great traditions of Christian religious life.

It is not surprising, then, that Abbot Geoffrey found Robert of Arbrissel a worrisome figure in need of correction. In keeping with his devotion to monastic ways, Geoffrey reprimanded Robert with a letter that contains several echoes of the Rule of St. Benedict. The abbot wrote in about 1107, several years after the foundation of Fontevraud. Geoffrey's concern here is Robert's relations with women, both his pastoral care for them and his ascetic practices of sleeping among them. Excessive intimacy, Geoffrey fears, poses a threat to Robert as a pastor and as a sinful soul. Robert has been unwise at best, and is furthermore insufficiently attentive to both female perfidy and female weakness in spending his nights among women, a practice Marbode had condemned a decade earlier, apparently to no effect.

Geoffrey understood women to be dangerous, and cites two of the Bible's harshest passages, Sirach (Ecclesiasticus) 9 and 25, in support of his view. Intent on demonstrating the folly of Robert's ways toward women, Geoffrey does not mention male disciples or arrangements for followers at Fontevraud and elsewhere. His charges, then, are less broad-ranging than Marbode's but more focused. Furthermore, the letter raises interesting questions about Robert's mission and behavior. Were women indeed the vast majority of his disciples, either because that was his intention or because they were especially drawn to him, or is it only the suspicious misogyny of an upright traditionalist ecclesiastic that gives this impression? Was Fontevraud Robert's compromise with opinion rather than the focus of his work? Geoffrey's estimate of women is clear (here as elsewhere), but what about Robert's? Does having women about him for purposes of mortifying the flesh constitute a kind of objectification, and was his mission to them ultimately geared to that purpose? No reply from Robert has survived, so it is impossible to say what effect, if any, such a scolding had on him; certainly Robert's life from before this letter to long after was all of a piece. Whatever Geoffrey's hopes, his professions of affection were apparently sincere: several years later Robert's Fontevraud and Geoffrey's La Trinité joined together in an association of mutual prayer, documented by an accord dating to 1114. In the end, Geoffrey found Fontevraud a worthy enterprise, perhaps because it was increasingly like a traditional Benedictine monastery, however troubling the behavior of its founder.

TEXT: Geoffrey of Vendôme, *Oeuvres*, edited by Geneviève Giordanengo (Paris, 1996), 148–150

Geoffrey, humble servant of the monastery at Vendôme, to his greatly beloved brother in Christ, Robert: to observe the due measure of discretion and to be content with the boundaries established by the Fathers [Prv 22:28].[1] You know, very dear friend, your charity[2] knows well, that to do anything to the contrary is an attribute of human imperfection, and to refuse to correct such action is a diabolical presumption. To do nothing other than what we ought is angelic perfection, which our condition cannot attain as long as we are here below. Therefore, so long as we lack angelic perfection, let us by no means share the devil's presumption. Accordingly, venerable brother, we have put what follows before you because a sinister report circulates and we have heard that you have done and still do certain things. From the depths of brotherly love we impress upon your simplicity that if the reports are true, you should not offer excuses but rather correct matters with all haste.[3]

We have heard that you show solicitude for the female sex, which you have undertaken to guide, in two ways absolutely contrary to each other, such that you far exceed the due measure of discretion in each way. Word has it you permit certain of the women to live with you too intimately, that you quite often speak with them in private, and even that frequently you do not blush to sleep among them at night. In this way, so you claim, you seem to bear worthily the cross of the Holy Savior when you attempt to extinguish fleshly ardor wickedly aroused.[4] If you do this now, or ever did it, you have discovered a new and unheard of but fruitless kind of martyrdom. Surely it can neither be made useful nor in any way fruitful, because it is a known presumption against reason. In fact you have presumed against reason in no small way if you have on any occasion slept with the women whom you should have stolen from the world in order to acquire them for the Lord—especially since it is prohibited by Solomon, the Holy Spirit thundering in him and through him: Do not lie down with a woman, nor be too solicitous of her, nor gaze at her, lest you are enticed into sin by her beauty and perish [Sir 9:3–5]. And again: Woman snatches precious souls [Prv 6:26] and her conversation lights up man's heart like fire [Sir 9:11].

Never rely so much on your faith, brother, that you believe you cannot fall if you do not walk carefully. The world is slick and muddy. Man could not stand firm in it for long; he fell quickly and rose with difficulty or not at all.[5] You, albeit in this world, have climbed a high mountain, so to speak, and have thereby turned people's eyes and tongues toward you. See to it that you, standing atop the peak, do not fall, nor through a martyrdom utterly unknown to the holy martyrs bequeath a mark of shame to the origins of religious life. Do not by any of your behavior cause scandal to the world, nearly all of which follows you. For the ruin of many would be graver damnation for you.[6]

You speak often in private to certain women, as rumor has it and as we said before, and by lying in bed with them you are tortured in a new kind of martyrdom.[7] With these women you always show yourself pleasant in speech and ready in action; you show every kindness, nothing spared. But with others, if ever you speak to them, you always appear too harsh in address, too severe in correction; you actually torture them with hunger and thirst and nakedness, all compassion forsaken.[8] If this is so, you offend greatly in each way, and exceed all due measure of discretion, for you behave too forgivingly toward the ones, too brutally to the others. You have begun to rule an exceedingly harsh realm, one that has very often led its ruler to death: *the origin of sin was made by woman* and through her all men die [Sir 25:33]. You must act so wisely and uprightly that the grace of compassion shows you to be a mother, correction to be a father to these women around you, and those who have no less perfection should have no less affection.[9] Not one of them should be cherished by you more than another, unless she has been found better. Offer a measure of compassion or correction according to the measure of merit or fault.

This especially should be fixed in your mind: in the Gospel the Lord says *Blessed are the merciful, for they shall obtain mercy* [Mt 5:7]. The feminine sex is quite fragile and delicate, and therefore it is necessary that it be ruled with the sweetness of compassion more than by excessive severity, lest it be *overwhelmed by excessive sorrow* [2 Cor 2:7] and he who ought to rule it be deceived thus by Satan. For a ruler is deceived by Satan if it happens that one who is to be ruled perishes through too much sorrow when he could have been saved through gentleness. Though out of compassion we exhort your goodness in this letter, we do not wish to take the action of justice away from you. We desire you to be equally just and compassionate. Therefore let your compassion reject inordinate pardon and your justice always have compassionate sympathy.

Farewell, and make us partakers, we fervently pray, in your holy prayers.

SUPPLEMENTAL BIOGRAPHICAL MATERIALS

1. The "Miracle of Rouen": Robert and the Prostitutes (twelfth century)

This short text appears to have been part of a collection of edifying stories kept at the monastery of Vaux-de-Cernay. This house near Paris, only about ten kilometers from Hautes-Bruyères, a daughter house of Fontevraud, was founded shortly after Robert of Arbrissel's death. Vaux-de-Cernay was a member of the monastic federation headed by the Norman abbey of Savigny, founded by Robert's fellow hermit-preacher and companion Vitalis of Savigny (ca. 1070–1122). Perhaps a member of Vitalis's congregation witnessed or heard about this "miracle" and had it memorialized at Vaux-de-Cernay. Historians have contested the authenticity of the document, but in several details—Robert's spare clothing, his preaching among all sorts and conditions of people, including prostitutes, his biblicism, the remarkable effect of his words, and his encouragement of retreat to solitude for religious purposes—it is in keeping with other accounts, laudatory and critical. At the same time, it is easy to understand why the abbesses of Fontevraud would have chosen not to broadcast this story, given the unusual aspects of their founder's ways disclosed by Bishop Marbode and Abbot Geoffrey. The story of Robert in a city brothel shows that his preaching mission, despite his preference for solitude, was urban as well as rural.

TEXT: Jacques Dalarun, *L'impossible sainteté: La vie retrouvée de Robert d'Arbrissel (v. 1045–1116), fondateur de Fontevraud* (Paris, 1985), 349

Robert of Arbrissel had been accustomed to go barefoot through streets and towns so he could attract adulterers and prostitutes to the medicine of repentance.[1] One day, when he had come to Rouen, he entered a brothel. Sitting down before the hearth to warm his feet, he was surrounded by whores, who thought he had come in to have sex.[2] But as he preached the words of life and promised them Christ's mercy, the prostitute who was in charge of the others said to him, "Who are you, you who say such things? Know full well that during the twenty-five years since I came into this house to perpetrate wickedness, never has anyone come here who spoke of God or made us trust in His mercy. Yet if I knew that the things you say are true, I swear to you by Christ, whom I have angered with innumerable sins, that I would freely renounce sin." Robert said to her, *"Have faith, my daughter* [Mt 9:22], and do not despair of His mercy, because if you renounce your sins and acquiesce to my sound guidance, you will without a doubt gain God's mercy." Upon hearing this, the madam, along with all those living there, prostrated herself at his feet, promising to renounce her sins and do penance in good works. Without delay, the holy man led them out of the city toward the wilderness and went out rejoicing with them, and once there he happily gave them the promised rewards.

2. Bishop Peter of Poitiers: On the Foundation of Tusson (1112)

This charter shows another instance of collaboration between Robert and his patron and protector Bishop Peter II of Poitiers. It concerns a challenge to Robert's possession of property donated by a pious lord for the foundation of a daughter house of Fontevraud. Robert proceeds by engaging the sympathies of laypeople as well as the bishop and cathedral canons of Poitiers. In the end, he obtained the assent of the monks who had claimed the property. Peter's charter, while explicitly stressing Robert's reputation as a holy man, also reveals a realistic and even cagey politician/diplomat, handling various people in different ways in order to attain his goal: a peaceful new settlement for his followers.

TEXT: PL 162: 1093–1094

I, Peter, by the grace of God bishop of Poitiers, want it known to all Catholics and declare by this writing on the present page,[3] that by means of careful procedure, for the honor of God and the observance of holy religion, the place commonly called Tusson was built with our assent and counsel and that of the canons of our see.[4] The site of Tusson, formerly abandoned in a great wilderness of forests and covered with a dense mass of thorns and brambles, was long uninhabitable. Nevertheless, some very old traces of a certain church were visible there.[5] And so a certain man of great religious devotion and good repute, Robert of Arbrissel by name, with careful attention sought out places isolated and suitable for divine worship in which he could establish the nuns he had gathered together to serve the living God. A certain nobleman called Fulk Frenicard came to Robert and with resolute entreaties urged him to deem it worthy to build a monastery in the aforementioned place. For Tusson was in his possession, and subject to his power.[6] Nevertheless the aforementioned Robert did not acquiesce immediately to Fulk's appeal, but proclaimed that he would build or receive neither this nor any other place in our diocese without our counsel and that of our clergy.[7] Therefore the aforementioned Fulk, ardently desiring to give Tusson to Lord Robert and the nuns who under his instruction served God most devotedly in the place called Fontevraud, came to us. He asked and pleaded that we grant the abovementioned place to the aforementioned man, Lord Robert, and that we beseech him to build a church there. Once these matters were settled, and when the said Robert, acquiescing to our insistence, ordered a church and other buildings be raised in that place for the honor of God and the observance of holy religion, the monks of Nanteuil claimed the property from him.[8] They said that the old church, traces of which were seen there (as it was reported above), was legally theirs. The monks' case was diligently investigated; since they were in no way able to show us that they had any possession or investiture in this church, nor did they hold any deeds to it,[9] we instructed Lord Robert that he should not desist from his undertaking.

But Robert, not wishing to accede to our commands, replied to us firmly that he was not about to do anything more at Tusson until the monks' claim was peacefully settled. Therefore, together with our clergy and Fulk Frenicard, we went to the monastery of Nanteuil, and in their chapter house we made an agreement with the abbot and monks of that place concerning the aforementioned claim.[10] For this agreement Fulk Frenicard gave the monks of Nanteuil four *sextarii* of grain in the tithe of Saint-Medard of Verteuil, which [parish] should pay them every year.[11] In the chapter house of Nanteuil, in our presence and with the advice and the assent of his monks, the abbot of Nanteuil, Gautier by name, completely dismissed and renounced this claim. And he granted the church of Tusson and the place itself in its entirety to Lord Robert and the aforementioned nuns and monks serving there, to be possessed in peace and in perpetuity. These matters peacefully settled by God's authority, we, with the counsel of our clergy, gave the place of Tusson along with its old church, whose traces, as was often said, are still there, to God and to Saint Mary of Fontevraud and Lord Robert and the oft-mentioned nuns, and we granted it so that they might hold it peacefully and undisturbed in perpetuity. We granted also on equal terms that all property that they might lawfully acquire in our diocese through the offering of the faithful would remain theirs, fixed and entire, in perpetuity. We declared as well that whoever presumes to disturb or disrupt this our ordinance, or rashly attempt to act against it, being warned off twice and thrice, should be held in the bond of excommunication until such time as he worthily makes satisfaction for the injury done.[12] Moreover, in order that this agreement and grant remain fixed and entire, in perpetuity, we have taken care to commit it to writing, and we have validated it with our own signature and ordered it to be secured with our seal. Present at this aforementioned agreement and grant were: William Radulph, master of the school of the Church of Poitiers; Peter of Saint-Saturninus, canon of that Church; Ademar, prior of the monastery of Nanteuil; Peter Fulcher, Humbert of Verteuil, Aimeric the Bright, Arnaud, Arrius, and many other monks of Nanteuil; Fulk Frenicard; his brother Ademar; Aimeric of Pindra; and many others, clergy as well as laypeople.

This agreement and grant was made in the chapterhouse of Nanteuil, in the year of Our Lord 1112, the fifth indiction, in the reign of Louis, King of the Franks.

3. Two Memorials of March 7th, 1116

These charters record events on the day of Robert's burial. The first is more specific than either *vita* about who was present. The text recounts the confirmation of Geoffrey of Blaison's donations to Fontevraud by his overlord, Count Fulk of Anjou. The impressive roster of mourners, including two archbishops and the powerful count, notably does not include Duke William of Aquitaine, never one of Robert's allies. The second, shorter charter recalls, many years later, the donation to Fontevraud of the nearby port of Rest, on the Loire near Montsoreau, and the toll-passage charged there. The port of Rest, near the confluence of the Vienne and Loire rivers, was a valuable property. Robert's burial in a priest's robes paid honor to his pastoral guidance at Fontevraud—likely Abbess Petronilla's choice for how people should see Robert for the last time.

TEXTS: *Grand Cartulaire de Fontevraud*, volume 1, edited by Jean-Marc Bienvenu (Archives Historiques du Poitou 63) (Poitiers, 2000), 445–446 (A) and ibid., 431–432 (B)

A. Charter concerning the properties of Geoffrey of Blaison (1116)

The authority of the fathers of old ordained that whatever is given to churches should be committed to the memory of letters lest it be lost in the mist of oblivion. Let it be known to all present and future that on the same day the body of Master Robert of Arbrissel, by the grace of God brought from far away, had been buried at Fontevraud, which he founded with God's help, a large crowd of religious people had assembled there for the funeral of such a great man. One of them was Leger, archbishop of the church of Bourges, another was Raoul, archbishop of Tours, along with Rainaud, bishop of Angers and many others, both abbots and priests without number.[13] Fulk the Younger, son of Fulk the count of Anjou, was there too, with innumerable people.[14] On that day Geoffrey of Blaison,[15] since he greatly desired the salvation of his soul, requested that Petronilla, abbess of Fontevraud, ask that the abovementioned Count Fulk himself confirm his assent, before the full chapter in the hearing of all, concerning all things Geoffrey himself had previously given to the church of Fontevraud for the salvation of his soul, that is, his houses, rents,[16] vineyards, and, not least, his daughters[17] and all things he seemed to possess in this world. Willingly hearing this request, the above named count satisfied the will of the abbess and the desire of the aforementioned Geoffrey, there in the chapter. Present at this agreement were Berlai of Montreuil, Gautier of Montsoreau, Robert of Blois, Gislebert of Loudun, and many other barons with a crowd of people.[18] In the year of Our Lord 1117,[19] in the reign of Louis, King of the Franks and William, Duke of the Aquitainians.

B. Charter concerning Rest (1134)

Let it be known to all present and future that Geoffrey Fulcrède gave to God and the church of Fontevraud the port of Rest and the rights of toll collection. And he did this in the hand of Master Robert of blessed memory and invested him with candles when he was dressed in priestly vestments before he was consigned to burial.[20] After eighteen years, William of Rest laid claim to the gift.[21] So Geoffrey gathered his court at Fontevraud, etc.[22] William himself dismissed the claim. These things were done in the presence of Petronilla, by the grace of God the first abbess of Fontevraud. Witnesses were: Geoffrey Rabaste, Geoffrey Landric, Philip of Bisaio, Sebrand, son of Simon of Saxe, Vitalis the Toll Collector, Fulcrède his brother, Raoul Bad Monk, Drogo of Montsoreau, Hubert of Val-Rusk, and many others.

4. Hildebert of Le Mans (?), Epitaph for Robert of Arbrissel (ca. 1116)

Hildebert of Le Mans is also known as Hildebert of Lavardin for his birthplace, north of the Loire not far from Vendôme. Born around 1056, Hildebert studied at the cathedral school of Le Mans and became both master of the school and, in 1091, archdeacon of the diocese—the same positions Marbode held at Angers. He was elected bishop of Le Mans in 1096 and quickly entered into a fierce quarrel with King William Rufus of England, who accused Hildebert of attacking his castle in Le Mans. Taken to England as a virtual prisoner, he returned in 1100 to preside over the rebuilding of his cathedral and to preach extensively in his diocese. In 1116, he invited the popular preacher Henry of Lausanne to Le Mans, in the interests of reforming his cathedral clergy, an entrenched and unspiritual group one of whom was known as Geoffrey Who Does Not Drink Water. In the bishop's absence, Henry led a revolt against the clergy and on his return, Hildebert had to work hard to reestablish control over them. (Henry of Lausanne was ultimately branded a heretic but succeeded, almost thirty years after the incident in Le Mans, in creating similar disturbances in southwestern France, quelled only with the help of the famed abbot Bernard of Clairvaux, a mentor of Robert's protégée Countess Ermengarde.) The elderly Hildebert was elected archbishop of Tours in 1125 and died in 1133.

His long and vigorous career as prelate notwithstanding, Hildebert is best remembered as a poet and member of the noted Loire Valley trio comprised of himself, Marbode of Rennes, and Baudri of Dol, the latter two by coincidence both represented here in their prose writings. Hildebert was one of the best Latin poets of the Middle Ages. He wrote on a variety of subjects religious and secular, and like Baudri he composed verses of praise and advice for Countess Adela of Blois. Nearly 100 of his letters to a variety of people have also survived, showing him to have been a capable theologian and political theorist as well as a refined literary stylist.

Many writings have been spuriously attributed to Hildebert, and the epitaph for Robert of Arbrissel may be one of them. However, Hildebert was an associate of Robert's and a fellow preacher who concerned himself with Fontevraud in his days as archbishop, so he may well have been the author of what follows. Short poems of this sort often were written for a peculiar kind of medieval document popular in the eleventh and twelfth centuries: the mortuary roll. At the demise of an especially beloved or distinguished person, a church or monastery sometimes dispatched a messenger to travel the countryside and stop at religious establishments to announce the death and solicit prayers. Members of the communities so informed wrote prayers and poems on parchments that, as they multiplied, were stitched together and rolled up. As its bearer traveled, the expanding document carried news and inspiration. One such roll, commemorating Abbess Mathilda of Caen, eventually recorded visits to more than 250 communities and was over sixty feet long. The roll of Vitalis of Savigny commemorates his frequent encounters with Robert of Arbrissel. One possibility is that the poem translated below was intended as part of a mortuary roll for Robert of Arbrissel, but such a document, if ever produced, has not survived.

In any case, the poem translated below is a dense and allusive tribute. The emphasis is on Robert's care of souls and his evangelism. His personal asceticism, a theme in other writings about him, also features here. The importance of his collaboration with Bishop Peter receives attention, once again. What goes unmentioned are Robert's monastic foundations and, indeed, any reference to his mission to women. Perhaps Hildebert, stung by the actions of Henry of Lausanne and aware of Robert's reputation for oddness, chose to remember his friend as a conventional holy man.

TEXT: PL 171: 1391–1392

The sower of God and heaven now reaps God and heaven.
They are abode and reward, God and heaven, for the good man.
This man was good, better than the good—I refrain from saying
best of the better. For praise it suffices to be good.
It was his way to strengthen faith and heal the heart,
to incite virtue and give hope to the guilty,
to root out sin, not extirpate sinners,
and to unite Christ, the head, to his members.[23]
He did not forestall hunger with food, nor thirst with drink,
nor cold with clothing, nor labor with rest.
He did not join his early and late meals by means of drink:
The man reined in appetite, not the other way around.
A hairshirt wasted away his sides, dry thirst his throat.
Hard hunger raked his stomach, wakeful care his eyes.
Rarely did he indulge himself with rest, even more rarely with
    food;
his gullet feasted on herbs, his heart on God.
He thirsted for water, but thirsted for more than water:
the cause of his twin thirst was Christ and the river.[24]
His flesh was worn down by the laws of Lady Reason[25]
and the laws had one savor: their savor was God.
Peter of Poitiers, who led his flock,[26]
Life made his equal in heart and death his peer in merits.
By reason of merit to those who have merited
is awarded what dear God gives and receives for each one,
and what each, beloved, gives and receives for God.[27]

AFTERWORD

Robert of Arbrissel's heart was buried at Orsan, and the rest of his body, as Andreas reported, was laid to rest by the altar in the nuns' church at Fontevraud, a handsome and substantial Romanesque edifice. Pope Calixtus II consecrated the building, still under construction, in 1119. Most of the people whose lives intersected with Robert's did not outlive him by very long. Archbishop Leger died in 1120 and was buried, as he had intended, at Orsan. If the biographer Andreas is also Prior Andreas, he was dead a few years later. The very aged Bishop Marbode returned to Angers from his see of Rennes to die at the monastery of Saint-Aubin in 1123; Baudri of Dol, who had likewise abandoned his diocese in Brittany, died in Normandy in 1130. Geoffrey of Vendôme died in 1132, his fortieth year as abbot of La Trinité.

The longest lived of those Robert knew best was Abbess Petronilla, who lived until 1149. Petronilla's leadership at Fontevraud lasted nearly fifty years. Under her guidance, Fontevraud became a socially and religiously prestigious head of a federation of monasteries for women, with men participating as sacramental providers and practical aides. The communities of repentant prostitutes and lepers soon disappeared. A generation after Robert's death, what had begun as an experimental community of religious seekers was essentially indistinguishable from other wealthy Benedictine nunneries. By the time of Abbess Petronilla's death, there were more than fifty daughter houses of the order, women's monasteries with co-resident communities of brothers.

The Order of Fontevraud grew more slowly after the death of

Petronilla, who was thereafter remembered at the abbey as "our incomparable and irrecoverable mother." At its height in the thirteenth century, the Order included about seventy monasteries in England, France, and northern Spain. Fontevraud became a favorite charity of the Plantagenets, the family who ruled as kings of England and lords over immense territories in France in the later twelfth century. Four members of the English royal family were buried at Fontevraud, including the legendary Eleanor of Aquitaine and her husband, King Henry II. Henry's aunt, in fact, succeeded Petronilla as abbess.

The memory of Robert faded rapidly after his death and had nearly vanished by the end of the Middle Ages. Interest was revived by Abbess Renée of Bourbon (1491–1534) and her five successors, all of them members of the French royal family. In about 1500, probably at Renée's behest, a brother of Fontevraud made a French translation of Andreas's *vita* of Robert. By the early seventeenth century, the nuns of Fontevraud were saying a weekly requiem Mass for Robert. A new tomb was made in 1622, with a sculpture portraying Robert in the priestly robes in which he was buried. The most active promoter of Robert's holy memory was Abbess Jeanne-Baptiste (1637–1670), who sponsored the publication of materials about Robert that are the basis for several of the editions translated here. This was part of a vigorous campaign at the papal court to have Robert made a saint—apparently the first such attempt since his death more than 500 years earlier. The abbess even sent two brothers to Vendôme, where they went so far as to remove from the original twelfth-century manuscript of Abbot Geoffrey's correspondence the folio containing the letter critical of Robert. The same censoring fate may have befallen the original manuscript of Marbode's letter to Robert, long preserved at Saint-Aubin in Angers. Fortunately, each letter had already been printed. Jeanne-Baptiste also had Robert's heart, which was said to have performed miracles at Orsan, brought to Fontevraud. Despite such efforts, Robert was not canonized in the early modern period.

Like all monasteries in France, Fontevraud was dissolved in the wake of the Revolution of 1789. In 1793, local villagers sacked the deserted cloister; it remained empty until 1804, when it was turned into a state prison. There was a rebirth of Fontevrist observance in the nineteenth century, which included the founding of a priory at Chemillé. In 1842, during remodeling of the abbey church to make more prison dormitories, it was discovered that Robert's tomb had survived the pillaging of 1793 and still contained his body and pastoral staff. The relics were given to the sisters of Chemillé. There followed another elaborately orchestrated attempt at canonization. It, too, ultimately failed. An examination of the tomb revealed that it contained the remains of not one but two bodies, Robert's and that of his patron Bishop Peter of Poitiers, apparently reburied together in 1622. Thus any miracles (of which a canonization case demands evidence) that occurred after 1622 could not be attributed to Robert alone. The neo-Fontevrist houses of the nineteenth century eventually disbanded. Robert's remains now rest in the Benedictine nunnery of Martigné-Briand in Anjou.

Although the twelfth-century abbey church of Fontevraud had been classified as a historical monument by the French government in 1840, it was not until 1963 that the compound stopped serving as a prison. In 1975 the entire monastic estate, its various parts erected between the twelfth and seventeenth centuries, came under the protection accorded historical sites in France. The abbey of Fontevraud, restored largely to its original condition, is now a tourist attraction and a cultural center hosting scholarly conferences.

There is still a small public devotional site for Robert in his native Arbrissel, where an old stone parish church, built perhaps in Robert's lifetime, houses a seventeenth-century wooden statue of him. Robert's story ends where it began, nearly a thousand years ago, in a village on the border of Brittany and Anjou. Robert of Arbrissel is not a saint of the Roman Catholic Church.

ENDNOTES

Notes to the Introduction

1. Fulk: *Grand cartulaire de Fontevraud*, volume 1, ed. Jean-Marc Bienvenu, 140 (no. 154); Abelard: PL 178: 357. The letters of Robert's critics Marbode of Rennes and Geoffrey of Vendôme are translated in this book.

2. The two most important studies of Robert of Arbrissel are Jean-Marc Bienvenu, *L'étonnant fondateur de Fontevraud, Robert d'Arbrissel* (Paris, 1981) and Jacques Dalarun, *L'impossible sainteté: la vie retrouvée de Robert d'Arbrissel (v. 1045–1116), fondateur de Fontevraud* (Paris, 1985). One chapter in Dalarun's study (pp. 119–150) describes the various interpretations of Robert over the last two centuries. In English see Berenice M. Kerr, *Religious Life for Women, c. 1100–c. 1350: Fontevraud in England* (Oxford, 1999), 15–63, especially pp. 20–30.

3. Much of this section summarizes current scholarly consensus about the period in which Robert of Arbrissel lived. Therefore I have not footnoted except in cases of specific and esoteric matters or controversial interpretations. An excellent brief treatment of France in the eleventh through thirteenth centuries is Constance B. Bouchard, *"Strong of Body, Brave and Noble": Chivalry and Society in Medieval France* (Ithaca, N.Y., 1998). For a compact and highly suggestive interpretation of Western Europe, with much attention to France, see R. I. Moore, *The First European Revolution, c. 970–1215* (Oxford, 2000).

4. See the essays in Theodore Evergates, ed., *Aristocratic Women in Medieval France* (Philadelphia, 1999).

5. The last few sentences recapitulate a generation of scholarly investigation whose results are well summarized in Constance B. Bouchard, *"Those of My Blood": Constructing Noble Families in Medieval Francia* (Philadelphia, 2001). Some of these conclusions are challenged in Evergates, ed., *Aristocratic Women in Medieval France*, esp. pp. 1–2.

6. Various aspects of the movement are discussed in Thomas Head and Richard Landes, eds., *The Peace of God: Social Violence and Religious Response Around the Year 1000* (Ithaca, N.Y., 1992).

7. On the movement and its manifold significance, see most importantly Giles Constable, *The Reformation of the Twelfth Century* (Cambridge, 1996).

8. For topics discussed in this paragraph and the next, see Colin Morris, *The Papal Monarchy: The Western Church from 1050 to 1250* (Oxford, 1989), 287–315. Morris finds it

"inconceivable that a regular preaching programme was taking place in country churches in the twelfth century" (p. 309).

9. Henrietta Leyser, *Hermits and the New Monasticism: A Study of Religious Communities in Western Europe, 1000–1150* (London, 1984).

10. Jaap van Moolenbroek, *Vital l'ermite, prédicateur itinérant, fondateur de l'abbaye normande de Savigny*, trans. Anne-Marie Nambot (Assen, 1990); Bernard Beck, *Saint Bernard de Tiron, l'ermite, le moine et le monde* (Cormelles-le-Royal, 1998).

11. There is an exception of sorts to this rule. The last two-fifths or so of Andreas's account of Robert's last months is known only through a late medieval French translation of the Latin original, as discussed in the introductory notes to Andreas's narration.

12. In Latin, the adjective *sanctus/sancta*, "holy," came to be a title of honor applied to certain people. The usage, then, was usefully ambiguous for writers, who could refer to someone as "holy" while implying the special category of recognized sanctity.

13. See the notes to Andreas's *vita* and Dalarun, *L'impossible sainteté*, 210–214.

14. On the process see M. T. Clanchy, *From Memory to Written Record: England, 1066–1307*, 2nd ed. (Cambridge, Mass., 1993).

15. All the authors of this potpourri of sources were male. This is not surprising, since the vast majority of attributed medieval writings are by men. In Robert's own time and place, however, there was a group of poet-nuns at the convent in Angers. Scholars are finding more and more evidence of female cultural patronage and accomplishment in the Middle Ages. Abbess Petronilla of Fontevraud probably had considerable influence on the form and content of the accounts of Robert by Baudri and Andreas, both of which she commissioned.

16. The documents, then, are not chronologically ordered. Those who want an idea of the kind of outrage Robert's peculiarities produced could turn first to Marbode's letter, which is also the earliest text.

Notes to Baudri of Dol, *First Life of Robert of Arbrissel*

1. In the medieval tradition, nuns are brides of Christ, hence Baudri's marital metaphor.

2. Baudri quotes God's instruction that Abraham depart from Haran, in the upper Euphrates River valley (in the east of present-day Syria), for a new homeland in Canaan, along the eastern Mediterranean. Like Abraham, Petronilla wandered for a time in search of a home.

3. *Seminiverbum.* The word is highly significant. Its lone appearance in the New Testament is Acts 17:18. The apostle Paul in Athens entered into debates with Stoic and Epicurean philosophers, that is, heirs to the great traditions of Greek thought. They referred to him, insultingly, as *spermologus* (translated into the Latin Bible most familiar in medieval Europe as *seminiverbius*). *Spermologus*, roughly "blabbermouth," was the term used by the Greek orator Demosthenes (384–322 B.C.) in his most famous oration, "On the Crown," to describe an enemy as a verbose and inane philosopher. Typical of early Christianity, the word was recast as a badge of honor for eloquent

preachers of the word of God. However, *seminiverb[i]us* was an unusual designation. It was usually applied to evangelists speaking to pagan audiences, as in the case of Goscelin's *vita* of St. Augustine of Canterbury, the "apostle of the English," whom Pope Gregory I (590–604) sent at the end of the sixth century to convert the Germanic kings and people of England (see PL 80: 79, 89). Robert, then, is likened to St. Paul and to the pioneers of European Christianity. Thus the word, used again by Baudri below, and also by Andreas, author of the second *vita*, may imply that Robert's audiences were not fully Christianized.

4. The theoretical ideal for all Christian monastics was virginity, and Baudri's references to Petronilla's marriage suggest that she was an unusual figure. This was not true, however; many nuns of this era had been (or were still) married. See Bruce L. Venarde, *Women's Monasticism and Medieval Society: Nunneries in France and England, 890–1215* (Ithaca, N.Y., 1997), 95–101.

5. In 1106, Pope Pascal II (1099–1118) issued the first bull offering papal protection to Fontevraud, at the suggestion of Robert's patron Bishop Peter II of Poitiers (1087–1115) (PL 163: 164). Bishop Peter was a longtime advocate who had gone to Rome in 1105 and met personally with the pope concerning Fontevraud among other diocesan matters. He remained a prominent patron of Robert and Fontevraud until his death less than a year before Robert's.

6. "The Fathers" are the great thinkers and writers of late antiquity (second through seventh centuries) like St. Jerome (ca. 340–420), who translated the Hebrew Bible or Old Testament and the Greek New Testament into Latin, producing the so-called Vulgate Bible, the version most widely read in the Middle Ages; or the brilliant and prolific St. Augustine of Hippo (354–430), author of the first autobiography in Western literature and originator of medieval political theory. Baudri's point is that if the distant genius of these people provides inspiration, so much more easily should the examples of distinguished Christians of his own time do so.

7. Vergil (70–9 B.C.) was the author of the epic poem *The Aeneid*; Cicero (106–44 B.C.) a great Roman lawyer, orator, and politician; these two were (and still are) considered master stylists of the Latin language.

8. This difficult passage seems to mean that the challenges of being a bishop in savage Brittany are doubled by the charge to write an account of Robert. In any case, Baudri emphasizes the absence of resources and abilities worthy of the task Petronilla has given him.

9. Sallust (ca. 86–35 B.C.) was a Roman historian whose works and style medieval writers admired.

10. Numbers 22–24 tells the story of Balaam, on a journey when his mount, an ass, briefly gains the power of speech at the Lord's command.

11. That is, the man/god Jesus.

12. Since the ninth century, the bishops of Dol had claimed archiepiscopal status, that is, ecclesiastical overlordship in the northwestern part of what was, according to the archbishops of Tours, part of their territory. (Just as bishops were chief priests, so archbishops were chief bishops.) Even before Baudri's arrival in Dol, the pope, recognizing the claims of the archbishop of Tours, had restricted the archiepiscopal pow-

ers of the see of Dol. Pope Pascal II had personally given Baudri the pallium, the cloth stole that symbolized an archbishop's jurisdiction, but limited the circumstances in which it could be worn. In Baudri's time and after, dioceses removed themselves from the authority of Dol and by the time Pope Innocent III declared that Dol was no longer an archbishopric in 1199, it had no subordinate dioceses left. At its largest, the archbishopric of Dol was, roughly, the region of Brittany, excluding the dioceses of Rennes and Nantes.

13. *Scolae Christianae doctrina.* The Rule of St. Benedict (see the introduction to this *vita;* a standard English translation is included in the bibliography) refers to the monastery as a school or company for the Lord's service, and it is probably this usage that Baudri, himself a monk, has in mind. A number of other passages in Baudri's sketch also recall the Rule of St. Benedict.

14. That is, there is much more to say about Robert's history *(rerum gestarum historia)* than Baudri will write. The author, concerned a few sentences ago with paucity of material, now finds that there is more than he can (or ought to) manage. Baudri's self-proclaimed ignorance, although a literary posture, may well reflect reality: there is no evidence of intimate friendship between the two men.

15. Obedience to Petronilla's charge in particular and to the duty to commemorate Robert in general. Baudri underlines the point when he refers to the process of writing as a "reply" in the next sentence.

16. *Christianae professionis cohaeres et filius.* As understood by commentators for centuries (including editors who have removed the phrase, considering it to reflect badly on the *vita's* subject), this expression indicates that Robert's father was a priest, and the wording suggests other relatives were priests as well. For rural clergymen to have wives and families, and for the priesthood to pass from father to son, was not unusual in premodern Europe. However, priestly celibacy was the ideal vigorously promoted, and largely imposed, by reformers during Robert's lifetime, so what was ordinary at the time of Robert's birth was a matter of dishonor or at least embarrassment by the time he died some seventy years later. Baudri calls Robert a *colonus,* a term with a range of meaning but certainly indicating that he was of soil-tilling, that is, non-elite background. Robert's origins, then, were in a farmer-priest family, a tradition he was likely expected to continue. The date of Robert's birth is nowhere stated but is traditionally thought to have been shortly before 1050; he was an old man, but apparently not of remarkably advanced age, when he died in 1116. A French translation of a funeral oration of Robert by Archbishop Leger of Bourges (on whom see Andreas's *vita*) says Robert was over seventy. But this late version of what may well have been an authentic text from 1116 is not reliable, since it refers to thirteenth-century events like the pontificate of Innocent III and the Albigensian Crusade (and is therefore not translated in this volume). It is possible that Robert was born five or ten years after the traditional date of 1045. See Bienvenu, *L'étonnant fondateur de Fontevraud,* 15–19; Bienvenu notes that Brittany was something of a Wild West, a turbulent borderland, in the eleventh century.

17. Arbrissel is thirty-five kilometers southeast of Rennes, the major city of Brittany. The village is in lower, that is, inland, Brittany not far from the border of Anjou,

in the eleventh century a more populous, wealthy, and orderly region to the south, comprising basically the lower Loire River watershed.

18. *Prout poterat*, a qualification that at very least suggests Robert's youth was not utterly devoid of sexual activity.

19. Could Robert find no sources of learning in his rural childhood home, or was he simply not very studious as a boy? Baudri's language is ambiguous. Clearly Robert developed a thirst for learning and a keen desire to pursue it far from Arbrissel, but the chronology, despite the author's claim a few sentences later, is very vague.

20. "France" here is not modern-day France but the much smaller region around the city of Paris controlled in Robert's student days by King Philip I. Although theoretically master of vast domains, the French king in the eleventh century was but one warlord among many, some of whom controlled much larger territories than he did. Brittany and Anjou had counts, and the counts of Anjou were particularly strong regional leaders in Robert's time. When Robert studied there, Paris was just beginning to attain its position as an intellectual center maintained ever since. Paris was a long way, geographically and culturally, from Arbrissel.

21. King Philip I of France, or "of the Franks," ruled from 1060 to 1108. Pope Gregory VII was elected in 1073 and died in 1085.

22. The wording echoes Jesus' command to render unto Caesar what is Caesar's and unto God what is God's (Mt 22:21, Mk 12:17, Lk 20:25).

23. Sylvester de la Guerche, member of a prominent family centered near Arbrissel, was an official in the court of the count of Brittany, elected bishop in 1076. This was a family tradition. Sylvester's great-grandfather Thibaud was a twice-married bishop in the late tenth century, succeeded by a son, then a grandson, then another son in the episcopal see. Between Thibaud's second son and Sylvester there was a bishop not of this family, but for nearly a century, there had been an episcopal dynasty at Rennes. Sylvester himself was a layman, apparently married although perhaps widowed by 1076, and his election was apparently effected through simony, exchange of money for ecclesiastical office. (The practice is named after Simon the Magician, who tried to buy from St. Peter the power of the Holy Spirit to work miracles: Acts 8:9–24.) Like clerical marriage, simony was not unusual but under largely successful attack by reformers in the late eleventh century; according to Robert's deathbed confession as recorded by his second biographer, Robert had participated in episcopal simony at Rennes, almost surely in the case of Sylvester (see Andreas's *vita*, section 41 and note). Bishop Sylvester was condemned for simony and incompetence and for a time deposed from office by a papal ambassador. He went to Robert in the late 1080s, perhaps under orders to cleanse his diocese of practices like simony and clerical marriage but unable to do so without cooperation from local clerical personnel, who were likely to have been resistant to change that reflected newly compelled ideologies of separation from secular society and practice. It is easy to see why cathedral and diocesan clergy would also have found Sylvester's reforming efforts hypocritical.

24. That is, Robert tried to enforce the newly urgent ideals of clerical celibacy and separation of the church from secular influence, as symbolized by simony. Inter-

estingly, Baudri's wording suggests that Robert was correcting himself as he corrected others; in other words, his years as archpriest of Rennes were important to Robert's spiritual development.

25. This rather feeble rationale suggests the more likely scenario: without the protection of his bishop, Robert was driven out of Rennes by those he had been charged to emend.

26. Angers, a city in the Loire Valley 100 kilometers southeast of Rennes, was the capital of the powerful counts of Anjou. The cathedral school of Angers, where Robert resumed studies, was headed by the poet Marbode, who several years later wrote the blistering critique of Robert translated below. Robert's study of *divina philosophia*, theology, was appropriate to a longtime student. He was already well trained in the traditional liberal arts curriculum and had moved on to advanced subjects. For Robert, the two years at Angers were an informal version of something like modern university graduate study.

27. *Eremum* here really means "wilderness," since there were no deserts in verdant Anjou. "Going to the desert" was the traditional expression to describe the choice to leave society on a solitary spiritual quest. The first such self-exile was St. Anthony (ca. 251–356), an Egyptian Christian who fled urban life for the literal deserts of his native land.

28. Baudri's metaphor combines elements from two Gospels. Luke 12:36 has Jesus commanding his apostles to be like good servants, waiting alertly for their master's return from the wedding feast. Matthew 25:14–30 is the parable of the talents, highlighting the need to return gifts with interest (mentioned in verse 27). Baudri may have conflated the two because in Matthew the parable of the talents is immediately preceded by that of the wise and foolish wedding attendants and because it is the Holy Spirit and His bride who speak in the passage from Revelation just quoted. Like many medieval writers, including Robert, Baudri was thoroughly conversant with the Bible and quoted it frequently, usually from memory, and thus often partially, loosely, or, as in this case, somewhat obscurely. *Talentum* meant both a measure of money and aptitude in medieval Latin, so Baudri's point is clear: the Lord will attend to His servant Robert's use of gifts bestowed by Him.

29. The model early Church was the community of Jesus' followers in Jerusalem after the crucifixion, whose common life is discussed in Acts 2:42–47 and 4:32–35. *Regula* is the term for any regulation concerning Christian life or practice, in this case applied to those who would participate in a structured religious life. *Regulares*, regulars, usually refers to those who lived such a life. Baudri carefully avoids the term "monk," which in his day most often designated men who followed the most famous *regula*, that composed by St. Benedict in the sixth century. "Canon" is a confusing term with a range of meanings, but here it refers to members of a religious community removed from secular society, like monks and nuns, but not so strictly separated from it, along the lines of the early communities of Jerusalem.

The house Robert founded was La Roë, about fifteen kilometers east-southeast of Arbrissel, on the border of Brittany and Anjou near the forest of Craon into which Robert had retreated. It was the first such non-monastic religious community founded in the archdiocese of Tours in at least 200 years. One of its most important early patrons and donors was the local lord Rainald of Craon.

30. Bees were proverbially wise and busy creatures. The Roman poet Vergil (see note 7 above) devoted scores of verses to their habits, and many medieval authors likened their heroes to wise bees.

31. Urban II (1088–1099), once a monk at the famous Burgundian house of Cluny, traveled in the French lands in late 1095 and early 1096. It was on this tour that the pope made his call for European warriors to head eastward in the First Crusade.

32. The abbey church of the monks of St-Nicolas at Angers was dedicated on February 10th, 1096. Robert preached to a crowd that besides the pope included Count Fulk IV of Anjou, at least four bishops and four archbishops, and numerous other ecclesiastical and secular notables.

33. *Et non insolitis mandat sermonibus uti.* The phrase might also mean "commanded him not to use unaccustomed discourse" and has been interpreted as meaning the pope was nervous about Robert's reputation for idiosyncrasy. Both grammar and situation argue against such an interpretation. *Non* and other negatives generally precede the word to which they especially apply according to the rules of Latin composition with which the highly cultured Baudri was familiar. Baudri also uses other emphatic double negatives in this *vita* (e.g., *non ignorabant* and *nec immerito*). It would also be odd for the pope to have selected a preacher he worried he could not trust for a great public occasion. Perhaps by some standards Robert's career was checkered—few in his day had been diocesan officials *and* self-denying charismatic hermits *and* founders of religious institutions by middle age—but in each of these pursuits Robert was in the mainstream of his era. Robert's truly unusual behavior was still in the future.

34. See note 3.

35. Robert was now dividing his time between supervision at La Roë and preaching that took him far afield. Baudri does not mention that during the visit to Angers, Urban II also supervised the further institutionalizing of Robert's foundation: the pope was present as documents were drawn up, in the days after Robert's public sermon, to confirm the donation of properties to La Roë for the support of the canons and to impose on them the so-called Rule of St. Augustine, a series of guidelines for religious life in community written by the great Church Father and frequently adopted by canons and canonesses in the Middle Ages. Robert's name appears in documents recording new donations of property and other business from the winter of 1096 to the spring of 1098.

36. That is, the command to preach. Robert apparently used the pope's charge as his reason to depart permanently from La Roë, where he was a leader but never, in any extant documents, designated by any formal title. However, it seems likely that Urban II had imagined Robert's life as that of a charismatic evangelist who toured from a base where he would lead the community of canons.

37. Here, halfway through the *vita*, is the first mention of Robert's desire to join together men and women in religious life. "Syneisactism," cohabitation of the sexes in common religious purposes, was an ancient Christian custom. Reflecting St. Paul's dictum that all are one in Christ (Gal 3:28), syneisactism in practice usually height-

ened awareness of sexual difference and sexual attraction while simultaneously deny-
ing the importance of difference and the lure of attraction. Robert was not alone in
the revival of syneisactism, but drew fierce criticism for practicing and sponsoring it:
see the letters of Marbode and Geoffrey of Vendôme, below.

38. Fount Evrald, Fontevraud, was hardly isolated, not the "desert" Baudri's description suggests. The fount or spring rose at the top of a valley four kilometers
south of the Loire. At the foot of the valley, on the river, lay Candes, site of the cell
(in medieval usage, a very small monastic community) where St. Martin, the monk,
evangelist to then-pagan Gaul, and finally bishop of Tours, had died in 397. Candes
was at the confluence of the Loire and Vienne rivers, a crossroads for traffic of people
and goods. (In Europe, water transport was faster and more reliable than that on land
until the coming of railroads in the nineteenth century.) Just downriver from Candes
was the castle of Montsoreau, the seat of a powerful local family who were early patrons of Fontevraud.

Although not remote, the site of Fontevraud was liminal because it lay near the
boundaries of ecclesiastical and secular territories. It is in the northern reaches of the
diocese of Poitiers, whose bishop Peter was an early patron of Fontevraud and may
well have suggested the site to Robert. The new community settled almost precisely
on the point of intersection of the dioceses of Angers (to the northwest), Poitiers
(to the south-southeast), and Tours (to the northeast), but removed from all three
episcopal cities. It is also on the borderland of the secular territories of Anjou,
Poitou, and Touraine. Robert's community, then, would be sheltered from overbear-
ing domination by powerful lords but also readily accessible to the world outside.

Again, Baudri gives no date. Robert most likely settled his band of followers at
Fontevraud in early 1101.

39. Medieval writers, following the Rule of St. Benedict, often used military life as
a metaphor for communal religious pursuits. Elsewhere Baudri refers to companies
and armies. In other documents the religious women and men of Fontevraud are said
to be *Deo militantes,* "fighting for God."

40. This sentence closely echoes chapter 48 of the Rule of St. Benedict (PL 66:
703–704; CSEL 75: 125–130), which dictates manual labor as a defense against the evil
of idleness.

41. The translation does not soften Baudri's harsh language of imprisonment and
slavery. These images reflect Robert's ascetic streak, but are also in keeping with contemporary metaphor: for example, the famed twelfth-century abbot of Cluny, Peter
the Venerable, referred to the monastery as a *gloriosum carcer,* a glorious prison.

42. Prayer and manual labor, usually agricultural work, were the traditional pursuits of Christian monastic communities. Robert assigned women entirely to
prayer—although there is no reason to assume he would have referred to females as
"the gentler and weaker sex"—and men to work. The contrast between active and
contemplative Christian lives is, once again, traditional: Robert's ideas were not new
and many were not unusual. Other traditional distinctions, like that between consecrated and lay people, Robert chose to elide.

43. *Magister* is how disciples address Jesus in the Latin Vulgate Bible. The word can
mean "master" in the sense of "leader" or "commander" but also "teacher." Both

meanings are implied here (as in the Gospels). That Robert eschewed other titles is significant: evidently he had no desire to find himself at the head of a community as he had at La Roë.

44. *Publicani et publicanae.* Publicans were tax collectors in the Gospels, examples of those set off from the community. In medieval texts the word (here in masculine and feminine forms) came to have the general meaning of "sinner" and was in the thirteenth century an epithet for heretics. *Publicanae,* the feminine form, also alludes to prostitution.

45. Robert in Baudri's description serves all three persons of the orthodox Christian Trinity of Father, Son, and Holy Spirit.

46. This vivid enumeration of the variety of women Robert attracted, as opposed to the single phrase devoted to men, suggests that the latter were in the minority. A document recording the original grant of land at Fontevraud mentions only "Robert and his company of religious women." A few lines further on, Baudri notes that the number of women made multiple dwellings necessary. Were men at Fontevraud from the start present largely to labor in service of women's prayer and contemplation?

47. From the beginning, local lords gave land and other property to the community, much of it already in use for farming. Baudri's rhetoric notwithstanding, the original grant of Fontevraud itself mentions a road and mills—this was hardly a dense wilderness. On Robert as the wise bee, see note 30 above.

48. Baudri's dense language here conflates two processes: first, Robert arranged the practical workings of a religious community of women and men together at Fontevraud; later, he established new monasteries along the same line in other places ("at a distance") as colonies from the mother house.

49. *In simplicitatem.* The word is a favorite of St. Paul in the Vulgate translation, where it means "integrity," "generosity," and "simplicity." Baudri implies the whole range of definitions here.

50. Medieval statistics are notoriously unreliable, and these figures are very high for a monastery or its dependent houses in the early twelfth century. On the other hand, the twelfth-century buildings that remain at Fontevraud are those of a sizeable religious community by medieval standards. It seems safe to take Baudri's word for it that there were a lot of people at Fontevraud.

51. Baudri portrays Robert's departure from Fontevraud as the result of the necessity to preach, implying that he was obliged to follow the papal charge of 1096. He left two women in charge. Hersende was the widowed mother-in-law of Gautier of Montsoreau, lord of a castle only a few kilometers from Fontevraud and an early patron of the house. She died sometime between 1109 and 1112. Petronilla was a scion of the lords of Craon, in northern Anjou not far from Arbrissel and La Roë. She was a cousin of Geoffrey of Vendôme, whose letter critical of Robert is translated below. Petronilla had been married to the lord of Chemillé, about sixty kilometers west of Fontevraud. Both women, then, had been married—in fact, it is not certain that Petronilla was not still married at this time. Robert chose them for their practical experience. Household and estate management was an important occupation of elite women in this era.

52. These *stipendia* for religious institutions usually took the form of regular cash

payments. The word sometimes refers specifically to poor relief, appropriate for the highly mixed community, including the desperate, described here.

53. *Incestas.* Baudri uses an adjectival form of this word in section 9, above, to describe the marriages of clergy and laity Robert assailed as archpriest of Rennes. Some of these women may well have been cast-off wives from clerical marriages now under attack.

54. Although Baudri has just referred to Fontevraud as a monastery *(cenobium)*, he is at pains to explain that this was, at least in these early times, no ordinary community, but one whose mission included prayer, pastoral care, and social welfare.

55. Robert, eager to avoid responsibility and commitment that kept him from his wandering evangelism, found himself nevertheless the oracle and champion of the diverse community of Fontevraud.

56. In John's Gospel, Nicodemus is a leader of the Pharisees who first approaches Jesus under cover of night for teaching and later helps Joseph of Arimathea, another secret follower, to entomb their master (Jn 3:1–22 and 19:38–42). Later, the Roman centurion (military officer) Cornelius has a vision in which an angel of God tells him to summon Simon Peter, the leader of the apostles. Peter in turn has just had a vision telling him that God will allow him to break Jewish law. Going to meet Cornelius and an assembled crowd, Peter realizes that preaching the Word to gentiles—which he proceeds to do—is what God meant by acceptable deviation from the law (Acts 10:1–43). Baudri indicates, then, that some women approached Robert in secret, others in full view.

57. These unspecific references to Robert's powers of healing and exorcism are strongly reminiscent of the accounts of Jesus' mission in the central portions of the synoptic Gospels of Matthew, Mark, and Luke.

58. The poverty emphasized here includes the notion of powerlessness, removal from worldly influence. Obviously material want at Fontevraud quickly vanished amidst the support Baudri describes.

59. The question of numerical accuracy aside, it is not clear who Baudri is counting. All at Fontevraud? All who lived there up to the time he wrote? All at Fontevraud and its dependent monasteries—here "cells," of which there were about a dozen by the time of Robert's death? Again, though, the general point is clear: Robert attracted many devotees and founded a number of monasteries besides Fontevraud in which they might worship.

60. A general remark on God's benevolence that recalls the manna provided to the Israelites through Moses (Exodus 16) and the few fishes and loaves that Jesus used to feed 5,000 people (Mt 14:13–21, Mk 5:30–44, Lk 9:10–17, Jn 6:1–13).

61. Baudri here uses the Greek adjective *dapsilôs.*

62. Baudri here makes the functioning of religious life a series of miracles; the last two wonders were in particular the responsibility of Abbess Petronilla.

63. King Louis VI (1108–1137); Pope Pascal II (1099–1118). Robert died on February 25th, 1116. The second *vita*, by Andreas, translated below, contains a detailed account of Robert's last months and last hours, and of the return of his body for burial at Fontevraud, to which Baudri devotes only a few sentences.

Notes to Andreas of Fontevraud, *Second Life of Robert of Arbrissel*

1. Andreas's intentions are clear: not to expand on Baudri's biographical narrative and encomium, but to tell more (if not all) about Robert's final months and death. Unlike Baudri's *vita*, this "treatise" *(tractatus)* centers on Fontevraud and Robert's arrangements for its future.

2. *Robertus, quasi roboratus vel robore certus.* This etymology is spurious, since Robert is a Germanic name, not a Latin one. (The actual meaning, "bright fame," would have served Andreas's purposes.) Finding significance in given names was in the Middle Ages, as now, a favorite pastime.

3. *Si quaeris scilicet, similis non invenietur/Qualis quantus erat fructu testante docetur.* It seems likely that Andreas was the author of this rhyme.

4. If the traditional date of ca. 1045 for his birth is correct, Robert was about seventy when Andreas picks up the story. That there is no comment on exceptional age suggests Robert had more or less lived out his biblical three score and ten years. By 1115, Robert had spent most of the last two decades in errant evangelism; it is not hard to imagine multiple chronic and incurable complaints that could plague an elderly man who had worked on the move for the last twenty years and who had cared little for his bodily needs. Robert's mission apparently never took him further than the west and north of what we call France, but the regionalism of Robert's era meant that anywhere outside familiar Anjou and Brittany was peopled with "foreigners."

5. Transfer from one community to another was a standard practice in medieval monasticism. However, in their reply, the monks (or almost all of them!) promise *stabilitas*, an ideal of remaining under the same rule that had been central to Christian monasticism from its origins.

6. The wording here closely echoes the Rule of St. Benedict, chapter 58 (PL 66: 803–806; CSEL 75: 146–151), on monastic profession.

7. Bishop Peter II of Poitiers, one of Robert's most important advocates and protectors in the early days of Fontevraud, had died in April of 1115. Robert's concern for permanent arrangements may well have derived in part from the death of his diocesan champion Peter. Medieval rulers liked to leave important ecclesiastical positions vacant for a period, since they often got the income accruing to the office until a new election. The indomitable William (VII of Poitiers, IX of Aquitaine, 1071–1126) had been denounced by Robert and his companion Bernard of Tiron at a church council in Poitiers in 1100 as "the enemy of all chastity and holiness." (On Bernard, see sections 13–18 and 73–74 and notes, below.) Count William is best remembered as the father of Eleanor of Aquitaine and author of numerous vernacular love poems that earned him the title of "the first troubadour." In 1114, Bishop Peter, who had repeatedly warned William to break off an adulterous liaison, excommunicated him in a public meeting. The outraged count chased the bishop out of the city into exile at nearby Chauvigny, where he died not long afterward, never having returned to Poitiers because he steadfastly refused to lift the excommunication. On Peter and his career, see George T. Beech, "Biography and the Study of Eleventh-Century Society: Bishop Peter II of Poitiers (1087–1115)," *Francia* 7 (1979): 101–121.

8. This peculiar appellation, *conversa laica*, refers to Petronilla's status as a relative newcomer to religious life after an adulthood in the world as a married woman.

9. It is not clear which text Robert is thinking of. Virginity was prized in Christian thought and life, but it was certainly not a requirement for election as abbess. Many early medieval abbess-saints had histories not unlike Petronilla's. Robert's words, or at least this report of them, reflects heightened Christian concern for sexual purity and perhaps anxiety about sexuality (especially female sexuality) that characterized this era.

10. In Exodus 40:12, the Lord instructs Moses to bathe his brother Aaron and Aaron's sons before dressing them in the vestments of priesthood for the sanctuary of the Ark of the Covenant—the sole use of *lotos*, the word Robert is quoted as using here, in the Vulgate Old Testament.

11. Another reference to the founding of the Hebrews' sanctuary; the Lord's instructions include eleven hair-cloth blankets as a cover for the Dwelling (Ex 26:7).

12. The image of a tabernacle's red interior glow protected by sturdy covering comes from the *Moralia in Job* (book 25, section 16: PL 76: 347; CCSL 143B: 1263) by Pope Gregory I (590–604), also known as Gregory the Great, a prolific author whose writings were widely read in the Middle Ages. The *Moralia* is a massive commentary on the biblical book of Job. In the passage recalled here, Gregory cautions against condescension toward those who labor for the material benefit (the sturdy covering) of the Church (the tabernacle aglow with color), an idea very much in keeping with Robert's argument.

13. In a Gospel passage Jesus tells the busy housewife Martha that her sister Mary has chosen the better part by sitting quietly at the Lord's feet. Martha and Mary became symbols for the active and contemplative lives, respectively, in medieval Christianity. On the changing interpretation of this story across the Middle Ages, see Giles Constable, *Three Studies in Medieval Religious and Social Thought* (Cambridge, 1995), 1–141.

14. Pope Urban II (1088–1099), who had met Robert at Angers in 1096: see Baudri's *vita*, sections 13–14.

15. That is, October 28th, 1115.

16. Petronilla, then, was among the early followers Robert had settled at Fontevraud fifteen years before the events described here.

17. The word *monogama* recalls 1 Timothy 3:2, where St. Paul demands that a Christian city elder—an early bishop—be *unius uxoris virum*, the husband of one wife. The wording here clearly echoes the papal decision concerning the four-times-married abbess discussed in the previous section.

18. It is not clear whether sections 7 through 9 elaborate on the description of the conference in sections 4 through 6 or refer instead to another gathering of ecclesiastical officials some weeks later.

19. Papal legates were agents of Rome. Since the eleventh century, popes had appointed local and regional ecclesiastical officials as, in effect, residential ambassadors. With Peter of Poitiers dead, Robert chose to appeal to Bishop Gerard, who used his direct ties to Pascal II (1099–1118) to obtain papal sanction of Petronilla's election. The document recording papal confirmation has not survived.

20. Robert's wishes in this regard went unfulfilled. Upon Petronilla's death in 1149

a longtime nun, Mathilda, daughter of Count Fulk V of Anjou, was elected abbess. With the exception of three abbesses who ruled in the years 1194–1210, Fontevraud was presided over by "claustral virgins" from 1149 until the abbey was disbanded in the wake of the French Revolution. For Robert's "other commands," discussed further in the following section, see the statutes translated below.

21. Chapter 55 of the Rule of St. Benedict (PL 66: 771–772; CSEL 75: 140–144) discusses monastic clothing and modesty of garb.

22. By 1115 there were about a dozen daughter houses of Fontevraud.

23. In 1112, King Louis VI (1108–1137) began building a monastery just west of Paris on the dowry lands of his stepmother Bertrade of Montfort, who had retired to Fontevraud a few years earlier. Louis acted in concert with Bertrade's relatives, powerful local lords. The new house was ready for settlement the next year and Bertrade joined the community shortly afterward. Bertrade had a very colorful life. The wife of Count Fulk IV of Anjou (1068–1109), she deserted him in 1092 for Louis's father, King Philip I (1060–1108), after Philip had repudiated his wife and Louis's mother, Queen Bertha. The liaison was an international scandal. For details, see Georges Duby, *The Knight, the Lady, and the Priest: The Making of Modern Marriage in Medieval France*, trans. Barbara Bray (New York, 1983) and sections 73–74, below.

24. The monastery of Bonneval is about thirty kilometers south-southeast of Chartres, along the route from Fontevraud to Hautes-Bruyères, Robert's destination. Bishop Ivo (1091–1115) was one of the most learned men of his time, an expert theologian and author of what was in the first half of the twelfth century the principal manual of canon (church) law. Ivo of Chartres wrote two short letters in the 1090s to a Robert who may have been Robert of Arbrissel. The letters encourage wise spiritual development and example but are sufficiently generic and uncertain enough in date that nothing connects them to Robert of Arbrissel with any certainty. The letters are in PL 162: 46, 49–50 and Yves de Chartres, *Correspondence*, vol. 1, trans. Jean Leclercq (Paris, 1949), 138–141, 152–157 (Latin texts with French translations).

25. This telegraphic recounting seems to mean the following: Robert was on the road to Hautes-Bruyères in late 1115 to install additional nuns from Fontevraud, accompanied by Abbess Petronilla and Prioress Angarde. (In monastic organization, a prioress or prior was second-in-command to an abbess or abbot. Some monasteries, especially subordinate daughter houses of an important abbey, had no abbot or abbess but instead a prior or prioress as the superior. This was the case for the daughter houses of Fontevraud, often called "priories.") Hearing about the longstanding dispute at Bonneval, Robert sent the nuns toward Hautes-Bruyères under the care of Angarde and then, along with Petronilla and his old ally Bernard, abbot of Tiron, headed off on a side trip to Chartres. Robert's contemporary Bernard of Tiron (ca. 1046–1117) was a fellow hermit, evangelist, and monastic patron. Unlike Robert, however, Bernard had settled young on monasticism, moving back and forth from monastic to hermit life in the diocese of Poitiers and adjacent regions. In 1114, he had founded the Benedictine monastery of Tiron with the help of the local bishop, Ivo of Chartres. Tiron is only about thirty kilometers from Bonneval; perhaps Bernard had already been invited to mediate the dispute.

26. The Latin of this passage is full of assonance: *destestandae dissensionis . . . postquam*

prudens concionator charitate conductus Carnotum advenit . . . *daemonicum discordiam funditus dissi-pavit.* Did Andreas have in mind future oral recounting of this anecdote? In monastic tradition, mealtime was often accompanied by the reading aloud of edifying material.

27. Ivo of Chartres died December 23rd, 1115. His successor, whom Andreas names just below, was Geoffrey of Lèves, who presided over the see (once Robert helped to get him securely installed) until his death in 1149.

28. The canons here are the clergy of the bishop's cathedral. The phrase *amissis suis facultatibus*, translated here as referring to lost property, could also mean that the canons were scared out of their wits. The count in question is Thibaud IV of Blois (1102–1152). The dramatic troubles recounted here were not unusual: often secular rulers wanted to participate in episcopal elections and sometimes annulled the cler-gy's lawful choices. There was also a tradition of pillaging a bishop's possessions after his death; the looting of the canons' dwellings recounted here is an example.

29. That is, the practice of obtaining ecclesiastical office in exchange for money, a practice Robert had fought as archpriest in Rennes decades earlier. Apparently posi-tions in the cathedral at Chartres were still being purchased in the time of Bishop Ivo.

30. Blois, on the Loire, was the capital city of Thibaud, a man with several titles referred to here as the count of Chartres. The prisoner, Count William II of Nevers (1097–1147) had taken the side of King Louis VI in a recent dispute and his imprison-ment was meant to discourage further hostilities against the powerful Count Thibaud. William ended his life as a monk.

31. *Charitas quae dividi potest nunquam vera fuit.* Working from memory, Andreas conflated two patristic texts. St. Jerome's letter to Rufinus notes, "Friendship that can end was never true friendship" *(Amicitia quae desinere potest vera numquam fuit)* (PL 22: 335; CSEL 54: 18). Augustine commented in a sermon that Jesus' tunic, which the soldiers who crucified him chose not to divide as they had the rest of his garments (Jn 19:23–24), is symbolic of "love that cannot be divided" *(charitas quae dividi non potest)* (PL 38: 149).

32. Berry is a region of west-central France. Robert's itinerary in his last months is impressive: from Fontevraud to Hautes-Bruyères via Chartres, back to Chartres, on to Blois and then to the priory of Orsan, which he left for a few days only to make his last trip back to it—a total of hundreds of kilometers. Andreas puns on the mean-ings of *talentum* just as Baudri did.

33. Orsan is fifty kilometers south-southwest of Bourges. Robert founded a monastery there in cooperation with the local lord Alard of Châteaumeillant, whose former wife, Agnes, had become a nun at Fontevraud. After their marriage was dis-solved by reason of consanguinity, Agnes became the first prioress of Orsan, around 1107.

34. Here Andreas introduces the first of several quotations and echoes of the writings of Sulpicius Severus concerning St. Martin of Tours (d. 397). Like Robert, Martin practiced both evangelism and eremitism. Sulpicius's account became the chief model for later hagiographers. For the phrase *O virum ineffabilem*, which comes from a letter about St. Martin's death and entered the liturgy for his feast day, see PL 20: 182 or CSEL 1:149.

35. Interestingly, the phrase *recto tramite* was often used from early Christian times as a metaphor for the monastic life that Robert himself never followed.

36. This could be a generic piece of religious self-criticism or may refer more specifically to difficulties at Fontevraud, perhaps including trouble enforcing the submission of men to women after Robert's death.

37. That is, Robert preached along the way.

38. Déols is about forty kilometers northwest of Orsan. The monks welcomed Robert there not only in light of his renown but in accordance with Benedictine traditions of hospitality to travelers.

39. *Seminiverbius:* see Baudri's *vita*, section 1 and note 3.

40. This is the duty of the abbot as defined in the second chapter of the Rule of St. Benedict (PL 66: 264; CSEL 75: 25). Again Andreas uses language that brings Robert closer to monastic orthodoxy.

41. The founder of Orsan: see note 33. An undated document, which may well refer to this agreement, shows the monks of Déols relinquishing their claim to property in Orsan to the nuns and Robert (PL 162: 1118). Perhaps the title to the property Alard had donated to found the house at Orsan had not been clear.

42. The first mention of Robert's companion in his last days, who was likely the author of the present account.

43. Graçay is about thirty-five kilometers northeast of Déols.

44. The third leg of what turned out to be a triangular itinerary, it is sixty kilometers from Graçay to Orsan. Issoudun is about halfway. Robert was quite determined to die among his sisters and brothers.

45. See note 33 on Prioress Agnes.

46. *Busnachias:* this very rare word could also mean little hamlets. In any case, Robert feared more banditry like that he had experienced only recently. Here is the first sign that Robert was aware that his body was to become an object of contention after his death—he worried that it would be stolen. The theft of holy relics was common in the Middle Ages: see Patrick J. Geary, *Furta Sacra: Thefts of Relics in the Central Middle Ages*, revised edition (Princeton, 1990).

47. Robert asks for communion on this Monday, February 21st, 1116, and again every day until his death on Friday, February 25th.

48. The lesson is that no Christian should approach the consecrated host for communion, the central ritual of the faith, without first examining the conscience and repenting sins and failures.

49. Archbishop Leger of Bourges died on March 31st, 1120. Since he was alive when Andreas wrote this paragraph, the second *vita* can be dated to no later than early 1120 and Baudri's *vita* previous to that—both within four years of Robert's death.

50. Bourges is fifty kilometers from Orsan.

51. *Villulam;* that is, the religious settlement at Orsan. The convent was never very populous, housing probably only a dozen or so religious women and men in 1116.

52. La Puye, in the diocese of Poitiers, was the site of a daughter house of Fontevraud founded about 1106. It is approximately 110 kilometers from Orsan.

53. *Sale condito sermone.* His public career as preacher ended, Robert continues on his

deathbed to preach to those who attend on his last hours, not without sharp admonition.

54. The chronology seems to be that Robert asked for Leger on Tuesday, February 22nd, and their meeting took place the next day.

55. The Burgundian Benedictine monastery of Cluny was famed for its wealth, the pomp of its ceremonies (to which Robert alludes), and the notable ecclesiastics it produced—among them the Pope Urban II who sent Robert on his preaching mission from Angers in 1096.

56. Actually, the expression comes from a well-known hymn in honor of Sts. Peter and Paul, who both died in Rome, attributed to Paulinus, bishop of Aquileia (d. 802).

57. That is, in the cemetery. As he proceeds to explain, Robert wants his grave to be accessible to the faithful, access to it not restricted to the residents of Fontevraud or any one group of them.

58. On Hersende, see section 21 of Baudri's account.

59. With these words, Robert anticipates his own posthumous reputation for sanctity.

60. *Ibi non est vita, ibi deest verus amor.* The sentence seems to refer to life on earth in mortal travail. But if the second *ibi* is a misreading for *ubi*, the meaning would be "There is no life there, where true love fails."

61. Robert repeats his earlier words of warning and supplication to Leger (section 32).

62. That is, the precious relic of Robert's holy corpse.

63. Orsan was built on Alard's property; see notes 33 and 41. Leger thinks that Robert's wishes may be hard to fulfill in light of the armed guard Alard and other local lords have stationed around the monastery, and is apparently no more eager than they to let Robert go.

64. Prioress Agnes appears unenthusiastic about interceding with her ex-husband and his fellow armed potentates for a cause that would remove Robert's body from her convent of Orsan.

65. The witnesses for this long prayer, as the next section makes clear, are the lay brother Peter and the priest Andreas, the probable author of this *vita.*

66. Robert adheres to Jesus' command to love and pray for enemies (Mt 5:44, Lk 6:27–35). It was surely not easy for Robert to pray for William, who had make the last months of his late patron Bishop Peter of Poitiers so difficult: see note 7 above.

67. In medieval iconography, a palm frond is the symbol of martyrdom. It was also the insignia of pilgrims to Jerusalem.

68. Neither of these is a biblical quotation or paraphrase. The first recalls another of Augustine's sermons in which the Church Father explains that contempt of the world and self-denial are a type of martyrdom and that death is not the only path to the martyr's palm (PL 39: 2159). Hildebert of Le Mans, whose poetic epitaph of Robert of Arbrissel is translated below, also touched on the theme in one of his monastic sermons. The second idea is an old one, perhaps dating to late antiquity and well established by Robert's time. The notion had its most famous exponent later

on in Thomas à Kempis, who wrote that since Christ's life was a cross, so should the life of any Christian be one.

69. Robert summarizes parts of the books of Genesis and Exodus, but adds other tradition that had grown up concerning Lucifer. See Jeffrey Burton Russell, *Lucifer, The Devil in the Middle Ages* (Ithaca, N.Y., 1984).

70. Robert's summary of the life and death of Christ stresses Jesus' humanity and redemptive purposes. This "affective" view of Jesus was characteristic of hermits, then monastics, in the eleventh century and was becoming widespread in the twelfth.

71. This brief reference appears to mean the following: when Robert was still a secular cleric, perhaps the parish priest of Arbrissel as heir to his father, he participated in an episcopal election tainted by simony. Given the chronology of bishops of Rennes, the bishop in question was almost certainly Sylvester de la Guerche, chosen in 1076 despite layman status. Apparently having undergone transformation while in office (he was deposed for a time by a papal legate, then restored to his office), this same Bishop Sylvester appointed Robert as reforming archpriest about a dozen years later. Perhaps it was complicity in this election and its unedifying early results that caused Robert to leave his native land for a long stay in Paris. See Baudri's *vita*, sections 7–10 and notes.

72. The French text preserves this speech in Latin.

73. The prioress of Orsan.

74. That is, a crowd of demons.

75. A mistake has crept in somewhere along the line; Andreas refers not to a letter by St. Hilary but to one by Sulpicius Severus describing the death of St. Martin of Tours (PL 20: 181–184; CSEL 1: 146–151), which text this whole passage echoes.

76. In Latin in the text: *Estote fortes in bello et pugnate cum antiquo serpente.* The line, an antiphon (liturgical phrase) to be said in celebration of the apostles, is attributed to Gregory the Great (see note 12). The text derives from Revelation 20:2, in which an angel defeats "the dragon, the ancient serpent, who is the Devil and Satan."

77. On Robert's sparing diet, dating to his hermit days in the 1090s, see Baudri's *vita*, sections 11 and 18. "Conversion" in medieval ecclesiastical language meant any change of life related to religion and most often referred to entry into monastic life. Here it refers to Robert's passage into his final mission, charismatic evangelism independent of the institutional ties that characterized the first several decades of his life from son of a parish priest to archpriest of Rennes.

78. That is, Alard's cooperation would be necessary for Robert's body to leave Orsan.

79. This address bears marked similarity to the beginning and ending of Robert's longer plea to Archbishop Leger in sections 31–34.

80. Raoul was the lay overlord of the region of the monastery where Robert made his last sermon (sections 22–24), Geoffrey probably Robert's host on the last night before his final return to Orsan (section 25).

81. When Alard will not promise to return the body to Fontevraud, Robert asks to be taken away from Orsan at once, which Alard forbids.

82. See Baudri's *vita*, section 1. Robert here mentions what Petronilla will repeat af-

ter his death: recourse to the power of the papacy in aid of returning Robert's body to Fontevraud. Pope Pascal II confirmed the rights and privileges of Fontevraud in 1106 and 1112.

83. Under pressure from Robert and Petronilla, Alard promises safe passage to Fontevraud, at the edge of Anjou, even though he fears repercussions in his own land when its dwellers find themselves bereft of Robert's holy body.

84. *Paratus sum ad opus familie sue quamdiu ipse jusserit militare.* This is a paraphrase from Sulpicius Severus's letter describing St. Martin's death: see note 75, above.

85. Following on the end of section 49, about the conflict between heart's desire and responsibility, Andreas emphasizes that Robert's preferred mission was solitary evangelism, but circumstances demanded supervision of others. The description of his life of contemplation and action echoes the reference to Mary and Martha in section 5; for similar remarks on the effect of his preaching see Baudri's *vita,* section 4.

86. "Est dit *veneris per sincopam,* c'est a dire venerable." The translator of Andreas's Latin was a bit confused, but the meaning is clear. In classical times, *dies Veneris* was one way to refer to Friday (the day being associated with the god Venus: "Venus's day"). Here Andreas suggests a new etymology: through syncope, the grammatical contraction of a word by the omission of letters in the middle, *dies venerabilis,* venerable for the reason Andreas explains in the next sentence, has become *dies veneris.* The etymology continues the implicit parallel of Robert of Arbrissel, preacher and spiritual guide, with Jesus Christ.

87. Here the French version retains the Vulgate Latin, as it does wherever quotations are italicized below in my translation.

88. A proverbial saying quoted in Latin: *Non progredi regredi est.*

89. Robert wants to ensure cooperation and communal decision making of men and women at Fontevraud and its daughter houses.

90. Robert's last words constitute a liturgical ceremony of penance and forgiveness. The *Confiteor* (so called for its first word, "I confess") is a general confession of sins. It was said on several occasions, in particular at the beginning of Mass or a private confession of sins. Absolution is a priestly prayer signaling remission for penitent sinners. The *Pater Noster* ("Our Father," called the Lord's Prayer by Protestants) is a version of the prayer Jesus taught his disciples (Mt 7:9–15, Lk 11:2–4), used at various times in Christian worship. Repeating the *Pater Noster* and other prayers was (and is) a common penance assigned after confession of sins.

91. As Robert foresaw, the struggle over his body began immediately upon his death.

92. Another quotation from Sulpicius Severus's account of St. Martin's death (see note 75), which became an antiphon for the celebration of Martin's feast day. The Latin was retained by the translator.

93. The battle lines have been drawn: the people of Berry were on one side, Petronilla and her charges on the other. Archbishop Leger has said he would consult with his clergy but apparently found it wise to include in the deliberations local lords—some of whom, after all, had armed guards at Orsan (see section 29). Given that it would gain his diocese the relic of Robert's body, and that violence had already

broken out once (section 55), how reluctant was the archbishop to deny his dying friend's heartfelt request?

94. The language reveals the tension of the scene: each side thinks the other's claim unjust and the threat of violence lurks. Evidently the nuns have gotten Robert's body back in their possession after it was taken from them to the bishop, although Andreas does not explain how.

95. Since it was February, this was a fairly dramatic gesture of propitiation and yearning.

96. Part of the theology of the removal of holy relics, called translation, is that the saint, as a living presence, will move or allow himself to be moved only if he so desires. In numerous accounts of the practice, the saint appears in a vision to an especially holy person to order the translation. The presumption here is that the holy dead Robert will participate in the process of returning his body to Fontevraud as he, while living, had requested.

97. The biblical reference here is to the rich youth's response to Jesus' admonition that he must divest himself of all his worldly goods to follow the Lord. Relying on the repeated words of their master and led by Petronilla, the party of Fontevraud defies the spiritual authority of the archbishop and the armed guard of local lords.

98. As with many medieval monasteries of any size, a village lay adjacent. It is not clear whether there was any such settlement before Robert located his followers at Fontevraud, although the place was certainly not the uninhabited wilderness Baudri's account (section 16 and note) suggests. A league is about four kilometers, approximately the distance from Fontevraud to Candes, the nearest village on the Loire (see next note). Andreas does not specify, but it is likely that the journey from Orsan was mostly by water, down the Cher River, which passes between Orsan and Bourges to where it meets the Loire near Tours, then down the Loire to landfall a few kilometers from Fontevraud.

99. Candes, at the confluence of the Loire and Vienne rivers, is where St. Martin had died in the year 397 (see note 38 to Baudri's *vita*). Here for the last time Andreas links Robert to the so-called "Apostle of the Gauls."

100. Lazarus is the patron saint of lepers, whose presence among Robert's followers the preacher recalled during his last illness (section 33, above), so this part of the settlement was almost certainly a leprosarium. See also Baudri's *vita*, section 22.

101. Who lived in the Madeleine is unclear. Its dedication suggests some were prostitutes such as Baudri noted were among Robert's followers. Perhaps the Madeleine was the residence of all converts to religious life who came to Fontevraud, the Great Monastery being reserved for the claustral virgins mentioned in section 5 above. The text of this sentence begins "The next day" ("Le jour d'après"), but that makes one night too many in this section for Robert's body to have arrived on Sunday and be buried on Tuesday. Given the insistence on female authority in this second *vita*, it would make sense that the body, after staying Sunday night in the main cloister, would be taken first to the leper house, then to the Madeleine, where it would stay over Monday night before presentation for public view and burial the next day. The addition of a day is likely scribal error at some point of transmission;

given how events are reported day by day in much of this *vita*, the slip is not surprising.

102. For a partial list of those present on the day of Robert's burial, Tuesday, March 7th, 1116, see the charter translated below.

103. Gregory the Great wrote the *Dialogues*, four large books of religious precepts and anecdotes in dialogue form. In the fourth book, Gregory teaches that burial in holy places can aid the salvation of those who died without grave sins, but that to bury the wicked there leads only to their greater damnation. He provides some examples, including stories of the bodies of sinners ejected from the churches in which they were buried, violently tossed out to the churchyard or incinerated in the tomb (PL 77: 412–421; SC 265: 176–185).

104. Tuesday evening, March 7th, 1116.

105. This was Archbishop Leger's oration: see note 16 to Baudri's *vita*.

106. See Matthew 3:1–5. John the Baptist's hairshirt was camel and his diet locusts and wild honey—arguably a less ascetic regime than Robert's.

107. St. Arsenius (354–450) was for some years a tutor in the imperial household of Constantinople. In middle age he fled to the deserts of Egypt in search of salvation. He lived for fifty-five years in mostly solitary asceticism and spiritual quest and is remembered for the copious tears he shed for his sins and those of the world. On Martha, see section 5 above. This whole paragraph compares Robert on equal terms with figures of the Old Testament, New Testament, and early Christian history.

108. Menelay, in central France, was a house of monks founded in the early Middle Ages.

109. All four Gospels recount a version of the story of the woman who tends to Jesus unbidden. Luke's account has her as a woman of ill fame whose sins Jesus forgives. In Luke 8, Jesus travels through Galilee accompanied by twelve male disciples and a number of women, some cured by Jesus—not unlike Robert, who in this anecdote has some nuns ("brides of Christ") with his party as he travels.

110. Robert apparently had less success against heretics than he did with the men of Menelay, since in Agen he resorts to excommunication. Southwestern France, in which Agen lies, became well known for its Christian heresies in the twelfth century. Robert's encounter with heretics was an early instance of tensions with authorities loyal to the Roman Church that led a century later to the Albigensian Crusade. No other details about the heretics Robert found in Agen survive. Andreas's motive in relating the stories of Robert at Menelay and Agen seems to be assertion of his subject's theological orthodoxy, which he may have thought advisable in view of Robert's idiosyncratic life and mission.

111. This section and the next are in brackets because they did not form part of Andreas's original Latin text. They derive in large part from the *vita* of Bernard of Tiron (see note 113) written some twenty years later by an author known as Geoffrey the Fat. The interpolator appears not to have had a copy of Geoffrey's text but had heard tell of it. It is impossible to know when this portion was added to Andreas's account; it may have been as late as the production of the French translation, which is the only surviving version of the final two-fifths of Andreas's *vita*. Nor is it clear who

added the material in the second half of section 74, which departs considerably from Bernard's biography. On Bernard of Tiron, see above, note 7 and sections 13–18.

112. On this matter and the parties involved, see above, notes 7, 23, and 25. The council took place in November 1100.

113. The twelfth-century Latin *vita* of Bernard of Tiron does not have Duke William acting on the king's behalf but instead afraid that a condemnation of his own sexual escapades would follow. Enraged, he ordered his men to rob, beat, and kill the assembled churchmen, who began to flee in all directions in search of safety. Amidst what Geoffrey calls shameful flight, only Bernard and Robert, "the mightiest defenders of justice," stood firm, courting martyrdom (PL 172: 1396; the latest edition is in Bernard Beck, *Saint Bernard de Tiron, l'ermite, le moine et le monde* [Cormelles-le-Royal, 1998], 312–479, at p. 364). The remainder of section 74 is a gloss on the *Life of Bernard of Tiron* rather than a retelling of it, with the exception of the final remark about martyrdom, which moves back toward Geoffrey's version.

114. Pierre de l'Etoile was another hermit and monastic founder, by 1100 abbot of Fontgombaud, fifty kilometers east-northeast of Poitiers. On Count William of Nevers, see section 17, above.

115. On Hautes-Bruyères, see section 12 and notes, above. The story here is very compressed, since Bertrade did not retire to Hautes-Bruyères until fourteen years after this council at Poitiers.

116. This is a paraphrase from Book III of Gregory the Great's *Dialogues* (PL 77: 313; SC 260: 426); see note 103 above. As often, Gregory wrote as if the end of the world were at hand.

Notes to Robert of Arbrissel's Writings

1. These striking formulations are adapted from a work of biblical exegesis called *Book of God's Promises and Predictions*, long attributed to Prosper of Aquitaine but now known to be the work of Archbishop Quodvultdeus of Carthage (d. ca. 454). In his commentary on the Hebrew Bible book of Tobit, Quodvultdeus remarks on seven evils and their even worse counterparts, pretense *(simulatio)* of contrasting virtues. Of the bishop's original seven pairs (after the seven demons Jesus drove out of Mary Magdalene [Lk 8:2]), Robert retained four—pride/feigned humility, envy/feigned love, greed/feigned mercy, lust/feigned chastity, and modified a fifth, intemperance/feigned moderation, to gluttony/feigned abstinence. The vainglory/feigned holiness pair (see Phil 2:3) is Robert's invention. Because his theme in this letter will be how to live a Christian life, Robert focuses on behavior and omits Quodvultdeus's more abstract pairs of mendacity/feigned truth and error/feigned faith. For the African bishop's text, see CCSL 60: 153.

The notion of seven (in some early schemes eight) deadly sins emerged in late antiquity and the early Middle Ages, the authoritative medieval list being pride, anger, envy, melancholy, avarice, gluttony, and lust. Of these, Robert omits anger and melancholy and adds vainglory, which the standard list merged with pride. The classic treatment is Morton W. Bloomfield, *The Seven Deadly Sins* (East Lansing, Mich., 1952).

2. It bears repeating here that, because there was no one "authoritative" version of the Latin Bible, the italicization that signals direct quotation gives only a rough idea of the balance between biblical quotation and biblical paraphrases, references, and allusions.

3. Robert refers to a view of scriptural interpretation common in the Middle Ages: the notion that any given passage can have multiple meanings. The distinction here is between allegorical and literal teaching.

4. Robert quotes or uses close verbal echoes of Jesus' Sermon on the Mount throughout this letter.

5. The source of the last two sentences is a collection of canon (church) law, the *Decretum* of Bishop Burchard of Worms, compiled in ca. 1025 and widely used in schools for a century. Specifically, they come from a chapter on the need to punish from the section concerning homicides (book 7, chapter 43; PL 140: 775–776). Apparently working from memory, Robert either forgot or decided not to note that the command to punish various malefactors originates with St. Jerome's commentary on Jeremiah, quoted by several authorities before Burchard repeated it. The idea attributed to St. Augustine by both Burchard and Robert in fact originates in the records of a church council in Marseille a century after Augustine's death; Burchard's wording is different. Nonetheless, the appearance of the two successive citations from the *Decretum* shows Robert had studied and remembered this collection of law.

6. See Matthew 22:37–40, drawn in part from Deuteronomy 6:5. In Robert's version, "yourself" *(te ipsam)* is in the feminine singular, reflecting his addressee.

7. This is not an exact quotation. In his writings, Augustine notes that whatever humans do faithfully—whether living a religious life or performing the spiritual correction of sinners—is to be done with love. The closest verbal echo to Robert's *Dilige et fac quodcunque vis* is in an Augustinian sermon: *Dilige et quidquid vis fac* (PL 46: 985). Along the same lines, Augustine also recommends saying whatever one says in loving spirit *(Dilige, et dic quod voles*: PL 35: 2144; CSEL 84: 134).

8. In the biblical book named after her, Esther is a Jewish woman who becomes queen to the Persian Ahasuerus (better known to history as Xerxes). While hiding her faith for fear of retribution, Queen Esther succeeds in foiling a court plot to execute all Jews in her husband's vast realm. After Esther reveals her origins, her triumph is commemorated by the establishment of the festival of Purim.

9. Apparently Ermengarde had sought to invalidate her marriage on grounds of consanguinity, blood relations considered taboo. In this era, clergy insisted on the indissolubility of marriage, but also considered as incest any marriage between people related within seven degrees of kinship or affinity (relations through marriage or godparenthood). In theory, such a system invalidated marriages between distantly related cousins—even those related only through marital or baptismal connection. A vast majority of marriages among the European elite violated these rules, violations "uncovered" when one or more parties to a marriage wanted to escape from it. In 1215, the papacy reduced the range to four degrees of prohibition to stem the tide of annulments. Ermengarde was certainly, by the twelfth-century calculation, incestuously joined to Count Alan, but she did not succeed in getting ecclesiastical judgment to

dissolve her marriage, which had produced three children and was, by the time of the writing of this letter, at least fifteen years long. On the marriage of Ermengarde's daughter in this light, see below, section 13.

10. The idea of a seeker in poverty following the similarly dispossessed Christ is proverbial; it appears to originate in a letter of advice from St. Jerome to a monk. The concept derives from Matthew 19:16–22, where Jesus tells a rich young man that to be more perfect he must sell everything he has and donate the money to the poor before joining the band of disciples.

11. Robert adds an interpretive phrase amidst his quotation of the psalm, suggesting demonic presence in Brittany.

12. The next quotation is not in the same place but a different Gospel; Robert recalls themes as much as discrete texts.

13. This is not the usual Vulgate language for this verse and the wording—*timentibus Deum nihil deest*—was used by Robert's sponsor Pope Urban II in his announcement of the First Crusade (PL 151: 568). Did Robert know of Urban's usage or hear it himself when he met the pope in Angers in 1096?

14. *Quibuslibet preciosis vestibus caro induatur, caro semper erit*, a reminiscence of Gregory the Great's remark in a sermon-commentary on the Gospels (*quibuslibet pretiosis vestibus induatur caro, quid est aliud quam caro?*: PL 76: 1126; CCSL 141: 94).

15. Genesis 6–9 (Noah), 12–25 (Abraham and Isaac), 25–50 (Jacob—although he never fled as far as Mesopotamia—and Joseph); Exodus 14 (Moses and the Red Sea); Joshua 1–12 (Joshua's victorious campaigns); 1 Samuel 16–31 (Saul and David); Genesis 19 (Lot); Daniel 1–3 (the three youths at the court of King Nebuchadnezzar of Babylon), 6:2–25 (Daniel and the lions).

16. An echo of part of the liturgy of the Mass.

17. Robert also instructed his followers to make this prayer immediately before his death: see Andreas's *vita*, section 54.

18. Robert decrees for Ermengarde the standard cycle of seven occasions of daily worship, known as the canonical hours. These were most closely associated with monastic life, for which they provided the framework, and the night prayers of Compline and Prime were probably of monastic origin. The hours in honor of the mother of Jesus are an addition; in this instruction Robert stresses female holiness and anticipates the cult of the Virgin Mary, which rose to prominence in the twelfth century. (Later medieval "books of hours," luxuriously decorated miniature manuscripts of which numerous examples survive, contained prayers to be said at the hours in Mary's honor.) In short, Robert encourages Ermengarde to organize her days around prayer.

19. By renewed reference to passages from Jesus' Sermon on the Mount, Robert offers a harsh critique of clerical practice.

20. In quoting the psalm, Robert changes the gender of the Latin adjective "needy" to suit his addressee.

21. In a somewhat confusing passage, Robert refers both to the marriage of Ermengarde to Count Alan, which she had tried to escape (see section 4, above) and that of her daughter Hedwig or Hawise. Hawise was engaged as a girl to Baldwin,

son of Count Robert II of Flanders. The union was challenged on grounds of consanguinity. Bishop Ivo of Chartres provided a genealogy showing that Hawise's great-great-great aunt had, nearly 150 years earlier, married Baldwin's great-great-great grandfather and thus the two were related in the sixth degree and their marriage incestuous (PL 162: 215–216). In remarking that the countess has consigned Hawise to death (if only passively, by allowing the arrangement to be made), Robert may have been less concerned about incest than about the young Baldwin's reputation for brutality. As Count Baldwin VII, this lord despatched ten disturbers of the peace in a creative fashion: he had the first nine in succession hang each other, then kicked out the stool on which the lone survivor stood. He also boiled a knight in a kettle for robbing a peasant woman of two cows. In any case, Robert urges Ermengarde to spare her daughter what she has suffered: an unfortunate marriage. Baldwin succeeded his father as count in IIII and the marriage, if it ever took place, was soon annulled; the count died childless from battle injuries in 1119. On Baldwin VII see Herman of Tournai, *The Restoration of the Monastery of Saint Martin's of Tournai*, trans. Lynn H. Nelson (Washington, D.C., 1996), 36–42.

22. Robert refers to monks, nuns, hermits, and recluses.

23. That is, the soul or, after 1 Corinthians 6:19, the Holy Spirit.

24. Genesis 3:1–13 (Adam and the apple), 25:29–34 (Esau's meal); 1 Kings 17:2–6 and 2 Kings 2:1–13 (Elijah's diet and ascent in the whirlwind); Jesus consumed fish and wine at numerous places in the Gospels. The first two allusions are to sin via simple foods, the third and fourth to the non-ascetic diets of holy men.

25. Interestingly, Robert refers to himself here as a priest, *sacerdos*, a word with very institutional associations.

26. Robert makes it clear that he wants the strong ascetic element which his flock imitates to survive in their monastic life. On Robert's care for his flock before the foundation of Fontevraud, see the critical remarks in the letter of Marbode of Rennes.

27. That is, according both to local understanding of what is just and according to the canons, the laws of the Christian Church. Priories of Fontevraud were established at La Puye in about 1106, at Lencloître and Guesnes a few years later.

28. A synod is any meeting of religious officials. The "Pentecost synod" alludes to a regular meeting of clergy of the diocese of Poitiers at the time of the Feast of the Pentecost, in the spring; the synod referred to below is the gathering of people from Fontevraud and the cathedral church of Poitiers to witness and sanctify the agreement this charter records.

29. To confirm their presence at this meeting, various officials of the cathedral clergy and two nuns of Fontevraud affixed personal marks or signatures. The accord of "all canons" and "all nuns" would presumably have been authorized before the meeting. On Hersende (d. 1109 or 1112) and Petronilla (d. 1149), the latter the first abbess of Fontevraud, see the *vitae* by Baudri and Andreas.

30. Saturday, July 19th, 1109.

31. That is, Robert makes a pure donation rather than an exchange or a sale.

32. The lands are located in southwestern France, about thirty kilometers east of Bergerac, just south of the Dordogne River.

33. "Fighting for God," a standard metaphor for monastic life in the Middle Ages, appears frequently in charters related to Fontevraud. "Lordly vassalage" extends the metaphor, making monks vassals of their Lord God.

34. Medieval religious women were frequently called *ancillae Dei*, handmaids or servants of God. But this usage is unusual. Since early medieval times, popes called themselves *servus servorum Dei*, "servant of the servants of God." The appellation *ancillarum Dei ancilla*, "handmaid of the handmaids of God," here applied to Petronilla, is very rare and appears to have been applied otherwise only to abbesses in the early Middle Ages. Petronilla was not yet an abbess: only several months after this document was written down did Robert appoint her as such (although his intention to do so may well be signaled by this usage). To make wordplay with an epithet for popes, more powerful and influential figures in the early twelfth century than ever before, in characterizing a nun seems audacious and might have been understood by some contemporaries as impertinent and disrespectful of papal office and authority.

35. Sunday, July 11th, 1115.

36. "Consul," the title of the chief official in the Roman Republic, is an appellation the counts of Anjou sometimes awarded themselves.

37. As with many charters reflecting property transactions, this one contains a list of witnesses, the patrons and neighbors of the monastery, sometimes identified by toponym, sometimes by profession, sometimes by sobriquet.

38. "Cloister nuns" are the veiled and virginal religious women to whom Robert refers in Andreas's *vita*, section 5. Although Andreas reported that Robert was worried about the competence of cloister nuns in practical matters, he imagined them sometimes involved with business. Silence is a standard monastic virtue: see the Rule of St. Benedict, especially chapter 6.

39. The notion is that gestures should not substitute for speech, as it often did in monasteries. Other twelfth-century critics complained that monastic hands could be as voluble and harmful as tongues. Robert desires to foster an atmosphere not just of communal spiritual pursuits, but one in which individual contemplation, like that he had sought in the "desert" of Craon, can be pursued without distraction.

40. This is a stricter diet than the one prescribed in the Rule of St. Benedict, chapter 39 (PL 66: 613–616; CSEL 75: 108–110), which allows the flesh of quadrupeds to the weak and ill.

41. That is, sacraments and healing rituals are to take place in community, and also, presumably, under the supervision of a priest, who as a man would not be allowed in the quarters of a sick nun.

42. This strong statement of Abbess Petronilla's authority, both its source and its extent, corresponds with Andreas's *vita*, sections 3–10.

43. Petronilla added the sixth stipulation and perhaps the seventh as well. The concerns are less internal matters of monastic behavior than the responsibilities of women at the head of what has become a substantial and geographically scattered monastic federation. The prioress, as second-in-command, is to have considerable authority for management among all monasteries of the order and at the death of the abbess will act in her stead until another is elected. Prioress Angarde is on the road with Petronilla in Andreas's *vita*.

44. That is, the customary series of daily prayers—what Robert recommended to Countess Ermengarde.

45. Personal poverty, the complete lack of private property, was a hallmark of medieval communal religious life, modeled after Jesus' apostles, who held all things in common (Acts 2:42–47 and 4:32–35). Possessions were, in Benedictine tradition, distributed by the superior, and that is what is to happen here: the women (presumably the abbess and prioress in particular, but other officials as well) are to distribute whatever the men will have.

46. Bleeding was a standard medical practice in the West in ancient times and remained so until the twentieth century. It was designed to balance the humors in the body for general good health, mental and physical, and was also a treatment for particular illnesses. Preventative care seems to have been its primary goal. Peter the Venerable, abbot of Cluny in the generation after Robert's death, corresponded with a physician on his regimen of bleeding as a way to strengthen generally fragile health. Bleeding was part of the monastic regimen since at least the seventh century. The ninth-century blueprint for an ideal monastery drawn up at the Alpine monastery of St. Gall included a special building devoted to bloodletting. In Robert's era, guides to monastic custom often prescribed a schedule for bloodletting: at Ely in England monks were to be bled every six weeks, while at other houses it was four or five times a year. Robert's stipulation, in keeping with his ascetic ways, allowed treatments relatively infrequent by contemporary monastic standards. See Walter Horn and Ernest Born, *The Plan of St. Gall* (Berkeley, Calif., 1979) 2: 184–188 and *The Letters of Peter the Venerable*, ed. Giles Constable (Cambridge, Mass., 1967) 1: 379–383 and 2: 247–251, 302–303.

47. Eating and living arrangements of men and women at Fontevraud were separate, but entire responsibility for poor relief and charity lay with the women.

48. That is, the brothers are not to accept "spiritual revenues," neither proceeds from the property of churches in which the laity worshiped nor the offerings of the faithful, the tithe or tenth of their income traditionally given the Church. Responsibility for oversight of parish churches, even if it did not include pastoral care, and the business of collecting tithes would take the brothers' concentration from their dependency upon and duty to the nuns.

Notes to Marbode of Rennes, Letter to Robert of Arbrissel

1. See Genesis 4:6–7. The language is not that of Jerome's Vulgate, but Marbode echoes the usage known to numerous patristic commentators on this passage, in which Yahweh chides Cain for sulking after his religious sacrifices are rejected, because evil lurks in such insolence. Shortly afterward, Cain kills his brother Abel. Christian theologians starting with Ambrose of Milan (ca. 340–397) interpreted *recte offeras sed recte dividas* as God's command not only to make appropriate religious offerings, but also make them in the right spirit and with righteous intention, not simply regarding sacrificial gesture as sufficient. Marbode probably knew the detailed explication in the work of Ambrose's most famous pupil, Augustine of Hippo (354–430), the most influential of all the early Church Fathers, in *The City of God* (book 15, chap-

ter 7). Robert would certainly have understood that Marbode's remark was meant to apply to the reader of this letter as well as the writer; the admonition to careful consideration of actions, with its implication that evil (in Genesis, fratricide) awaits those who do not heed it, sets the tone for what follows. On Augustine, see also note 13 below. This interpretation of Marbode's reference, and several others that follow, differ from the readings of Guy Devailly, "Marbode de Rennes et Robert d'Arbrissel," *Mémoires de la société d'histoire et d'archéologie de Bretagne* 57 (1980): 163–170.

2. Marbode refers to Robert's new "profession," his papally sanctioned preaching. "Appearance and deportment" translates *habitus*, which implies attitude, behavior, and appearance. Marbode has chosen the word carefully. Metaphorically, Robert has gone beyond the traditional garb of Greek philosophers in his uncommon practices, which the bishop finds objectionable in their attention-getting novelty. On Robert's appearance, see below.

3. Cherubim, an order of angelic spirits, are so described in Revelation 4:6, drawing on Ezekiel 1:4–28. In Ezekiel the creatures constitute a chariot, which leads Marbode to his next biblically derived remark in the following sentence.

4. The biblical *quadriga*, or four-wheeled chariot, of Aminadab (see Song 6:11) was interpreted in numerous ways by patristic and early medieval theologians, but only in the eleventh century, it appears, did it come to symbolize the four Gospels together, the sense in which Marbode uses it. A slightly later stained-glass illustration (ca. 1150) of the *quadriga* survives in the basilica of St-Denis near Paris. St-Denis is important as the first church in what became known as Gothic architectural style. Within a few decades, Gothic overtook the Romanesque designs characteristic of the time of Marbode and Robert, of which the abbey church at Fontevraud is an outstanding example.

5. *In quo genere quondam peccasti.* This enigmatic remark certainly suggests that Robert had a sexual history. The phrase might also be translated "with which gender you once sinned," and Marbode probably intended a double meaning. See Baudri's *vita*, section 7.

6. Marbode's meaning becomes clearer below: in order to tame the flesh, Robert puts sexual temptation directly in his path, which arouses suspicion that this is simply a cover for licentiousness.

7. Syneisactism, the close association of men and women in chaste religious communities with strong overtones of ascetic temptation and denial of carnal impulses, dates to the early history of Mediterranean and Celtic Christianity. According to Marbode, Robert accentuated the ascetic denial element of the tradition. On the practice and its condemnation in the early Church, see Dyan Elliott, *Spiritual Marriage: Sexual Abstinence in Medieval Wedlock* (Princeton, 1993), 3, 32–38. Jo Ann Kay McNamara frames her magisterial survey of women's monastic experience in Roman Catholicism from late antiquity to the twentieth century around the theme of syneisactism. McNamara sees the pluralist impulse to join men and women in religious pursuit as a way of recognizing spiritual equality consistently thwarted by male clerical hostility: *Sisters in Arms: Catholic Nuns through Two Millennia* (Cambridge, Mass., 1996).

8. *Per xenodochia et diversoria.* A xenodochium is a house for the sick, the poor, or

travelers under religious supervision. Apparently, before the foundation of Fonte-vraud, groups of Robert's followers had gathered informally in several places. Such informal spiritual communities, before and after Robert's time, were often regarded with suspicion by ecclesiastical authorities, especially if they included women. See Venarde, *Women's Monasticism and Medieval Society*, 40–47, 57–82 passim, 177–179.

9. The passage refers to Eve's disobedience of God's command when wheedled by a crafty serpent (Genesis 3) and also to what Christian theologians call "original sin." In the sentences that follow, Marbode elaborates on the theme, essentially equating women with snakes.

10. The line about asps is not from the Bible but a tract called *De singularitate clericorum*, which Marbode cites extensively below. The authentic biblical reference also follows in Marbode's source (PL 4: 840).

11. The first half of this verse from Proverbs notes that a prostitute goes much cheaper, for the price of a piece of bread. Marbode would have expected Robert and other readers to recall the comparison, an echo of the charges of debauchery explicit in this part of the letter.

12. *Ne te captura tua captivet*, intentional Marbodian wordplay.

13. The authorship of *De singularitate clericorum*, "On clerical celibacy," remains uncertain, although its attributions to the Church Fathers Cyprian of Carthage (to whom the treatise has been most often ascribed), Origen, and Augustine are certainly incorrect. The most accessible edition of *De singularitate clericorum*, which is more about general dangers of too close association of men and women than the special calling of priests, is PL 4: 835–870. On the treatise, its history, and its authorship, see Adolf von Harnack, *Der pseudocyprianische Traktat "De singularitate clericorum," ein Werk des donatischen Bischofs Macrobius in Rom* (Leipzig, 1903). Harnack makes a careful (if ultimately circumstantial) historical and philological case for the authorship of Macrobius, a North African priest of the schismatic Donatist sect, later its leader in Rome from ca. 340–ca. 370. If Harnack is right, Marbode's lengthy quotation is ironic: it quotes a renegade Catholic of late antiquity to criticize someone whose life and work take him to the margins of Catholic orthodoxy. Perhaps following Marbode, the theologian Philip of Harvengt (ca. 1100–1183) also credited the tract to Augustine, as did late medieval manuscript copies of the treatise. It is quite possible that Marbode himself first decided the piece, anonymous in the only surviving manuscript that predates the present letter, was an authentic work of Augustine. Whatever the truth of authorship or attribution, Marbode has chosen appositely to quote from a diatribe on the dangers of syneisactism (see note 7). The quotation here is at PL 4: 841.

14. Jerome, Letter 52 (PL 22: 531–532; CSEL 54: 423). Jerome (ca. 347–420), translator of the Vulgate Bible, makes these remarks in a letter on the duties of priests and monks. Marbode is quoting from memory here, so the language does not match Jerome's after the first verbatim phrase. The same is true for many of the quotations from classical and patristic authors that follow; I have noted only important mistakes or manipulations.

The stories to which Jerome refers are in the Hebrew Bible books of Samuel and 1 Kings. David, ruler over the united kingdoms of Israel and Judah, committed adultery with Bathsheba, arranged his troops in a battle to ensure the death of her husband, and then married her himself. God's punishment was the death of David and Bathsheba's firstborn. The next king, David and Bathsheba's son Solomon, displeased God by allowing some of his 700 wives and 300 concubines to weaken his devotion to his ancestral faith. Angered that Solomon built temples for foreign religions at his wives' request, God told Solomon that his punishment will be posthumous: the kingdom assembled by his father will splinter after his death.

15. Marbode could mean that even eunuchs for the kingdom of heaven (see Mt 19:12), that is to say those who have voluntarily renounced sex, still struggle with lustful thoughts, or that they are tempted to other means of physical gratification.

16. There are several references to burning straw in the Hebrew Bible; Marbode is probably thinking of the book of Isaiah, which twice uses the metaphor to refer to the ease with which Yahweh will destroy those who disregard his will (5:24, 33:11), once to describe the fate of the magicians and seers who cannot save the daughter of Babylon from destruction (47:14).

17. The lengthy quotations from *De singularitate clericorum* (see note 13) are interesting for two reasons. First, Marbode quotes no other text at such length in the present letter. Secondly, there is none of the reworked syntax, that is, slightly imperfect reproduction, that characterizes Marbode's other quotations. In this case, then, the bishop had a copy of the text at hand, and thought it so relevant and persuasive that he duplicated several sentences of it, albeit reordered to suit his purposes.

18. Seneca, *Epistles* 14.14. The letter collection of this Roman public servant and Stoic philosopher (ca. 4 B.C.–65 A.D.) made him second in popularity only to Cicero of the ancient pagan authors in twelfth-century Europe. Marbode's quotation puts him in the early stages of a Senecan revival: see L. D. Reynolds, *The Medieval Tradition of Seneca's Letters* (London, 1965), 101–124. In light of Marbode's letter, Reynolds's statement (p. 103) that Berengar of Tours is the only eleventh-century writer to quote from Seneca's letters is incorrect, but this second quotation from the Loire Valley strengthens the case that the widespread diffusion of Seneca's works may have had its source there. There is a twelfth-century copy of Seneca's letters from the monastery of Saint-Aubin, where Marbode died in 1123, in his native Angers (Angers, Bibliothèque municipale, ms. 298).

19. Jerome, Letter 52 (PL 22: 535; CSEL 54: 430); see note 14.

20. The text of the sixteenth-century edition is defective here and no subsequent reconstruction is satisfactory, so I have omitted a sentence. In its mangled form, it appears to ask if observers would not draw the wrong conclusions about more important matters given Robert's insouciance in lesser ones.

21. Again, Marbode equates eccentricity and insouciance with arrogance by putting in Robert's mouth the claim that he is like the preacher who baptized Jesus (see Matthew 3 and 11:2–15).

22. This passage is an example of Marbode's careful manipulation of biblical language to his own rhetorical purposes. Here Marbode's words closely echo James 3:11—*numquid fons de eodem foramine emanat dulcem et amaram aquam*, "When ever did a spring give out sweet water and salt from the same opening?"—with the significant

addition of the phrase *contra naturae ordinem*. That addition recalls Romans 1:26, where the apostle Paul condemns same-sex erotic behavior as *contra naturam*, "against nature." Additionally, Marbode recasts the metaphor James used by emphasizing *foramen*, "opening" or "hole," and eliding *fons*, "spring." Perhaps drawing also on the sexually charged usage of *foramen* in Song of Songs 5:4—*dilectus meus misit manum suam per foramen et venter meus intremuit ad tactum eius*, "my beloved thrust his hand through the hole and my womb trembled at his touch"—Marbode returns to the topos of sexual chaos with which he began and raises the stakes by a suggestion of further deviance. On the development of a rhetoric of condemnation of male-male sex by theologians, in a critical stage of intensification in the eleventh century, see Mark D. Jordan, *The Invention of Sodomy in Christian Theology* (Chicago, 1997).

23. In Ephesians 4:22, Paul urges his converts to put off the *veterem hominem*, the old self that belonged to their former wicked ways. The next few adjectives recall, again, the sin of sexuality and the disobedience from which it came in the Garden of Eden. The grammar is intentionally ambiguous, making the sentence condemn both Robert and his least charitable detractors by not identifying which of the two parties under discussion is backwards, earthly, and diabolical.

24. The rural parish, the region around a church served by a resident priest, had emerged as a unit of rural society in Western Europe in the tenth century, but most parish priests of Marbode's time lived little better than the agrarian peasantry to whom they ministered. Pastors who served rural Christians were distinguished from their flocks only in their level of education, and even that was often rudimentary. Priests celebrated mass and presided over the births, deaths, and marriages which were the most dramatic human events for the illiterate and sometimes hungry people they served. In theory, the Christians of a parish supported the church and its works with tithes (a tenth of their earnings, in cash or kind) or first-fruits, the first garnering of the harvest offered ritually. See Leopold Genicot, *Rural Communities in the Medieval West* (Baltimore, 1990), 90–107.

In practice, peasants often had enough trouble feeding themselves and their families, so the parish priest was often an agricultural laborer supporting himself (and any dependents: despite repeated prohibitions from the eleventh century forward, clerical marriage and concubinage were common in the countryside throughout the Middle Ages and beyond. For one example of sixteenth-century rural life in which the majority of the Catholic faithful saw nothing unusual or irregular about their pastor as a family man who worked beside them in the fields, see Marc R. Forster, *The Counter-Reformation in the Villages: Religion and Reform in the Bishopric of Speyer, 1560–1720* [Ithaca, N.Y., 1992], 20–27.) Marbode's charge, then, is a serious one: he sees the livelihood of straitened local guardians of the faith to be threatened by Robert's charisma and the devotion it inspires. The accusation has additional force in light of Robert's own origins.

25. *Honores*. In medieval usage, this word has a variety of meanings, including positive moral traits, fidelity, high social rank, ecclesiastical office, property, lordship, and other signs of honor, including monetary reward. All these are implied here.

26. As often in Marbode's quotations, there are some minor differences from the

received text, here Gregory the Great's letter to the bishop of Naples (PL 77: 1082–1083; CCSL 140A: 835–836).

27. Marbode refers to a monastic or canonical rule *(regula)*, e.g., of St. Benedict or St. Augustine. He returns to the risk of nonregular religious life in section 30, below.

28. Here Marbode imitates his classical models with the rhetorical device of preterition, in which announcing the omission of a subject draws attention to it. On the small medieval religious houses called "cells," see Baudri's *vita*, section 16 and note 38.

29. The language is that of imprisonment and escape. Marbode implies that Robert has, through his insouciance, consigned many naive and innocent women to shame, misery, and desperation.

30. Amidst the graphic metaphorical extension of Jesus' reasoning about the risks of plunging headlong into new practices, Marbode's wordplay juxtaposes *uter*, "wineskin" with *uterus*, "womb."

31. Marbode refers to the house of canons Robert had founded at La Roë, which he left permanently in order to preach shortly before this letter was written.

Notes to Geoffrey of Vendôme, Letter to Robert of Arbrissel

1. Geoffrey declares his themes at once. Discretion, *discretio*, is a key characteristic of the ideal abbot in the Rule of St. Benedict to which Geoffrey was so devoted; its opposite is *praesumptio*, presumption, mentioned several times. (Interestingly, Bishop Marbode urged the same quality on Robert in section 31 of his letter, perhaps quoting chapter 64 of Benedict's Rule [PL 66: 882; CSEL 75: 166] in finding discretion the mother of virtues.) The novelty of Robert's practices seems an unnecessary breach of tradition, ways of the past in general suggested by the quotation from Proverbs and the example of the Fathers of the Church, the monastic saints Benedict and Gregory the Great in particular. Geoffrey says, in effect: be like me, a wise abbot. Robert's first biographer Baudri stressed that Robert did not want to be an abbot.

2. *Tua dilectio*, a title of respect.

3. Geoffrey's technique is the same as Marbode's: he avoids direct accusation by framing his complaint as a collection of rumors, and implies that Robert's innocence and sincerity *(simplicitas)* are undermined by a fatal lack of prudence.

4. Robert, then, tempts the flesh in order to mortify it. Such an ascetic practice, however unusual and liable to misunderstanding, is not out of character according to the accounts of the critic Marbode and both of Robert's sympathetic biographers. On hermits and women, see Dominique Iogna-Prat, "La femme dans la perspective pénetentielle des ermites du Bas-Maine (fin XIᵉ–debut XIIᵉ siècle)," *Revue d'histoire de la spiritualité* 53 (1977): 47–64.

5. These two sentences recall Genesis 2–3, when God made Adam from mud only to see him fall from grace through disobedience.

6. Geoffrey echoes Marbode's charge of demagoguery.

7. The verb is *cruciare*, which means to crucify as well as to torture or torment. Geoffrey uses it again below to refer to Robert's treatment of his female followers.

8. *Omni relicta pietate. Pietas* has a great range of meanings in medieval Latin, from duty to charity to compassion to piety. Geoffrey's usage of this heavily freighted word (for consistency's sake translated as "compassion" throughout this letter) is intentional.

9. Geoffrey counsels a dual parental role for Robert: motherly kindness and fatherly discipline. On the parental roles of abbots, see Caroline Walker Bynum, "Jesus as Mother and Abbot as Mother: Some Themes in Twelfth-Century Cistercian Writing," in *Jesus as Mother: Studies in the Spirituality of the High Middle Ages* (Berkeley, Calif., 1982).

Notes to Supplemental Biographical Materials

1. The notion that sin was a wound to be healed with the medicine of repentance or penance was proverbial.

2. The language is quite candid: *meretrices* assume Robert has entered *causa fornicandi.*

3. Bishop Peter draws attention to the use of writing to memorialize events. A society that had worked to a significant extent through oral transactions was in transition toward the literate, bureaucratic systems to which modern Westerners are heir.

4. Tusson is seventy-five kilometers south-southwest of Poitiers, near the border of the diocese of Angoulême. The canons here are the clergy of the cathedral, the bishop's church, in Poitiers.

5. Such places were not uncommon in Western Europe in this era, after centuries of mobility and periodic economic and military disturbances.

6. In this world characterized by decentralized power, a relative lack of good written record, and large stretches of uninhabited or thinly peopled landscape, ownership of a given place was often a matter of dispute. Fulk claims possession and authority, but the document stops short of saying he actually *owns* the land in question. On concepts of land possession and ownership in this period, different from our own Roman law-derived notions, see Barbara H. Rosenwein, *To Be the Neighbor of Saint Peter: The Social Meaning of Cluny's Property, 909–1049* (Ithaca, N.Y., 1989), esp. 109–143 and Constance B. Bouchard, *Holy Entrepreneurs: Cistercians, Knights, and Economic Exchange in Twelfth-Century Burgundy* (Ithaca, N.Y., 1991), esp. 178–181.

7. That is, the cathedral canons, who shared supervision of diocesan property.

8. Nanteuil is a monastery in central Poitou, about twenty kilometers from Tusson.

9. Again, Peter lays stress on the written word; the argument that arises here shows how charters or other documents could be used. "Investiture" is the putting of a person or institution in possession of something, in this case probably referring to a lord's grant of a church formerly in his control to a monastery. Churches in lay control were one target of papal-sponsored reform in this era, with its overall concern for separating the things and people of the church from those of the secular world. Churches and the properties that went with them to support clergy were often under the control of monasteries in the Middle Ages.

10. The chapter house was the room in which monks and nuns assembled to discuss various matters secular and spiritual. Outsiders attended meetings there for business purposes. The next document also records business done "in chapter."

11. On tithes, see the Introduction and the Statutes of Fontevraud. A sextarius is a dry measure, strictly speaking a sixteenth of a peck, but standards varied widely. Verteuil-sur-Charente is between Nanteuil and Tusson, where Fulk was evidently lord with rights over at least one parish church.

12. Excommunication is the removal of a person from the community of the church, and thus, at least in theory, from the Christian community in general. It included a withholding of the sacraments held necessary to salvation.

13. On Leger of Bourges, see Andreas's *vita*. Raoul of Orléans was archbishop of Tours 1087–1118, Rainaud of Martigné bishop of Angers 1102–1124. The see of Poitiers, in which Fontevraud lay, was still vacant after the death of Bishop Peter nearly a year earlier.

14. Fulk V, count of Anjou 1109–1129 and brother of Countess Ermengarde of Brittany, was called Fulk the Younger to distinguish him from his father.

15. Geoffrey was the lord of Blaison, between Fontevraud and Angers on the banks of the Loire, about forty kilometers northwest of Fontevraud.

16. *Census*, so possibly "taxes" instead of or as well as rents. In any case, it was standard for a lord to promise regular monetary payments to a religious house as well as donating real property.

17. Two or more of Geoffrey's daughters, then, became nuns at Fontevraud. Gifts at entry into religious life, for male and female postulants, were common in this era, although there was increasing concern that this was a form of simony: see Venarde, *Women's Monasticism and Medieval Society*, 100–103, 114–115, 163.

18. Like the donor Geoffrey of Blaison, Berlai was another neighboring lord. On Gautier of Montsoreau, a longtime patron of Fontevraud, see Baudri's *vita*, section 21 and note. Loudun was about thirty kilometers away in Poitou, Blois much more distant, up the Loire River beyond Tours. All these witnesses except Robert of Blois appear in other early charters as patrons and protectors of Fontevraud.

19. A scribal error, since Robert was buried on March 7th, 1116.

20. That is, he put Robert in symbolic possession of the property by placing candles in the hands of his corpse. Dozens of other charters of the period 1101–1115 record the donation of property to Fontevraud *in manu domini Roberti* or *in manu magistri Roberti*, into the hand of Robert. Even dead, Robert remained the emblem of Fontevraud.

21. This charter, then, records the settlement of a claim in 1134.

22. *Et cetera* here probably means that Geoffrey brought witnesses, his "court," who remembered his acts of eighteen years earlier and testified to them. Memory remained important even in the age of record.

23. That is, join together the head and body of the Church. For the idea of Christ as head of the Church and the faithful as its body, see Ephesians 5:22–30.

24. These two dense and enigmatic lines appear to suggest that Robert's bodily thirst was less than the thirst for the waters of baptism the preacher inspired. In the

second line, Hildebert writes *unda*, a word he uses elsewhere to refer specifically to the water of the River Jordan, in which John the Baptist blessed Jesus, and to connote consecrated baptismal water in general.

25. Reason was a central concern of Hildebert's writings, an aspect of his so-called Christian humanism.

26. Which flock is unclear, perhaps purposefully. Peter, with whom Robert made the pact translated above, was the bishop of Poitiers and as such a regional chief pastor. He was also, however, a patron of Fontevraud, which represents an aspect of Robert's career Hildebert otherwise chooses to overlook.

27. *Per meritum datur emeritis quod dat recipitque / Gratus utrique Deus, gratus uterque Deo.* The density of Latin poetic expression here means that English requires more than twice as many words to translate it.

BIBLIOGRAPHY

Beck, Bernard. *Saint Bernard de Tiron, l'ermite, le moine et le monde.* Cormelles-le-Royal, 1998.

Beech, George T. "Biography and the Study of Eleventh-Century Society: Bishop Peter II of Poitiers (1087–1115)." *Francia* 7 (1979): 101–121.

Benedict. See *Rule.*

Biblia Sacra Iuxta Vulgatam Clementinam, 6th edition. Edited by Alberto Colunga and Laurentio Turrado. Madrid, 1982.

Bienvenu, Jean-Marc. "Les deux *vitae* de Robert d'Arbrissel." In *La litterature angevine médiévale,* 61–76. Paris, 1981.

————. *L'étonnant fondateur de Fontevraud, Robert d'Arbrissel.* Paris, 1981.

————. "Les premiers temps de l'ordre de Fontevraud (1101–89). Naissance et évolution d'un ordre religieux." Thèse de doctorat d'Etat. University of Paris, Sorbonne, 1980.

Bloomfield, Morton W. *The Seven Deadly Sins.* East Lansing, Mich., 1952.

Bond, Gerald A. *The Loving Subject: Desire, Eloquence, and Power in Romanesque France.* Philadelphia, 1995.

Bouchard, Constance B. *Holy Entrepreneurs: Cistercians, Knights, and Economic Exchange in Twelfth-Century Burgundy.* Ithaca, N.Y., 1991.

————. *"Strong of Body, Brave and Noble": Chivalry and Society in Medieval France.* Ithaca, N.Y., 1998.

————. *"Those of My Blood": Constructing Noble Families in Medieval Francia.* Philadelphia, 2001.

Bynum, Caroline Walker. *Jesus as Mother: Studies in the Spirituality of the High Middle Ages.* Berkeley, Calif., 1982.

Le cartulaire de l'abbaye de Cadouin. Edited by J.-M. Maubourguet. Cahors, 1926.

Chédeville, André, and Noël-Yves Tonnerre. *La Bretagne féodale, XIᵉ–XIIIᵉ siècle.* Rennes, 1987.

Clanchy, M. T. *From Memory to Written Record: England, 1066–1307,* 2nd edition. Cambridge, Mass., 1993.

Constable, Giles. *Letters and Letter-Collections* (Typologie des sources du moyen âge occidental, fasc. 17). Turnhout, 1976.

————. *The Reformation of the Twelfth Century.* Cambridge, 1996.

————. *Three Studies in Medieval Religious and Social Thought.* Cambridge, 1995.

Corpus christianorum. Continuatio medievalis. Turnhout, 1966–.

Corpus christianorum. Series latina. Turnhout, 1953–.

Corpus scriptorum ecclesiasticorum latinorum. Vienna, 1866–.

Dalarun, Jacques. *L'impossible sainteté: la vie retrouvée de Robert d'Arbrissel (v. 1045–1116), fondateur de Fontevraud.* Paris, 1985.

Devailly, Guy. "Marbode de Rennes et Robert d'Arbrissel." *Mémoires de la société d'histoire et d'archéologie de Bretagne* 57 (1980): 163–170.

Dictionary of the Middle Ages. 13 volumes. New York, 1982–1989.

Duby, Georges. *The Knight, the Lady, and the Priest: The Making of Modern Marriage in Medieval France.* Translated by Barbara Bray. New York, 1983.

Dunbabin, Jean. *France in the Making, 843–1180,* 2nd edition. Oxford, 2000.

Elliott, Dyan. *Spiritual Marriage: Sexual Abstinence in Medieval Wedlock.* Princeton, 1993.

Evergates, Theodore, ed. *Aristocratic Women in Medieval France.* Philadelphia, 1999.

Forster, Marc R. *The Counter-Reformation in the Villages: Religion and Reform in the Bishopric of Speyer, 1560–1720.* Ithaca, N.Y., 1992.

Geary, Patrick J. *Furta Sacra: Thefts of Relics in the Central Middle Ages,* revised edition. Princeton, 1990.

Genicot, Leopold. *Rural Communities in the Medieval West.* Baltimore, 1990.

Geoffrey of Vendôme. *Oeuvres.* Edited by Geneviève Giordanengo. Paris, 1996.

Gold, Penny Schine. *The Lady and the Virgin: Image, Attitude, and Experience in Twelfth-Century France.* Chicago, 1985.

Grand cartulaire de Fontevraud, volume 1. Edited by Jean-Marc Bienvenu. (Collection des archives historiques du Poitou 63.) Poitiers, 2000.

Guillot, Olivier. *Le comte d'Anjou et son entourage au XIe siècle.* 2 volumes. Paris, 1972.

Halphen, Louis. *Le comté d'Anjou au XIe siècle.* Paris, 1906.

Harnack, Adolf von. *Der pseudocyprianische Traktat "De singularitate clericorum," ein Werk des donatischen Bischofs Macrobius in Rom.* Leipzig, 1903.

Head, Thomas, and Richard Landes, eds. *The Peace of God: Social Violence and Religious Response Around the Year 1000.* Ithaca, N.Y., 1992.

Herman of Tournai. *The Restoration of the Monastery of Saint Martin's of Tournai.* Translated by Lynn H. Nelson. Washington, D.C., 1996.

Horn, Walter, and Ernest Born. *The Plan of St. Gall.* 3 volumes. Berkeley, Calif., 1979.

Iogna-Prat, Dominique. "La femme dans la perspective pénetentielle des ermites du Bas-Maine (fin XIe–debut XIIe siècle)." *Revue d'histoire de la spiritualité* 53 (1977): 47–64.

Ivo of Chartres. See Yves.

Jaeger, C. Stephen. *The Envy of Angels: Cathedral Schools and Social Ideals in Medieval Europe, 950–1200.* Philadelphia, 1994.

Jessee, W. Scott. "Robert d'Arbrissel: Aristocratic Patronage and the Question of Heresy." *Journal of Medieval History* 20 (1994): 221–235.

Jordan, Mark D. *The Invention of Sodomy in Christian Theology.* Chicago, 1997.

Kerr, Berenice M. *Religious Life for Women, c. 1100–c. 1350: Fontevraud in England.* Oxford, 1999.

Leclercq, Jean. *The Love of Learning and the Desire for God: A Study of Monastic Culture.* Translated by Catharine Misrahi. New York, 1961.

The Letters of Peter the Venerable. Edited by Giles Constable. 2 volumes. Cambridge, Mass., 1967.

Leyser, Henrietta. *Hermits and the New Monasticism: A Study of Religious Communities in Western Europe, 1000–1150.* London, 1984.

Library of Latin Texts [CD-ROM]. Turnhout, 2002–.

McNamara, Jo Ann Kay. *Sisters in Arms: Catholic Nuns Through Two Millennia.* Cambridge, Mass., 1996.

Marbode of Rennes. *Incipit liber Marbodi.* Edited by Yves Mayeuc. Rennes, 1524.

Moolenbroek, Jaap van. *Vital l'ermite, prédicateur itinérant, fondateur de l'abbaye normande de Savigny.* Translated by Anne-Marie Nambot. Assen, 1990.

Moore, R. I. *The First European Revolution, ca. 970–1215.* Oxford, 2000.

Morris, Colin. *The Papal Monarchy: The Western Church from 1050 to 1250.* Oxford, 1989.

The New Catholic Encyclopedia. 18 volumes. New York, 1967–1988.

Patrologia cursus completus. Series latina. Edited by J.-P. Migne. 221 volumes. Paris, 1844–1864.

Peter the Venerable. See *Letters.*

Petigny, Jean de. "Lettre inédite de Robert d'Arbrissel à la comtesse Ermengarde." *Bibliothèque de l'Ecole des Chartes* 15 (1854): 209–235.

———. "Robert d'Arbrissel et Geoffroi de Vendôme." *Bibliothèque de l'Ecole des Chartes* 15 (1854): 1–30.

Porter, J. M. B. "Fontevrault Looks Back to Her Founder: Reform and the Attempts to Canonize Robert of Arbrissel." In *The Church Retrospective: Depictions and Interpretations* (Studies in Church History 33), edited by R. N. Swanson, 361–377. Woodbridge, 1997.

Reynolds, L. D. *The Medieval Tradition of Seneca's Letters.* London, 1965.

Rosenwein, Barbara H. *To Be the Neighbor of Saint Peter: The Social Meaning of Cluny's Property, 909–1049.* Ithaca, N.Y., 1989.

The Rule of St. Benedict. Translated with introduction and notes by Anthony C. Meisel and M. L. del Mastro. Garden City, N.Y., 1975.

Russell, Jeffrey Burton. *Lucifer, The Devil in the Middle Ages.* Ithaca, N.Y., 1984.

Smith, Jacqueline. "Robert of Arbrissel: *Procurator mulierum.*" In *Medieval Women,* edited by Derek Baker, 175–184. Oxford, 1978.

Sources chrétiennes. Paris, 1941–.

Venarde, Bruce L. *Women's Monasticism and Medieval Society: Nunneries in France and England, 890–1215.* Ithaca, N.Y., 1997.

Walter, Johannes van. *Die ersten Wanderprediger Frankreichs: Studien zur Geschichte des Mönchtums.* 2 volumes. Leipzig, 1903–1906.

Werner, Ernst. *Pauperes Christi: Studien zu sozial-religiösen Bewegungen im Zeitalter des Reformpapsttums.* Leipzig, 1956.

Yves de Chartres. *Correspondence,* vol. 1. Translated by Jean Leclercq. Paris, 1949.

Robert of Arbrissel: A Medieval Religious Life was designed and composed in Centaur by Kachergis Book Design, Pittsboro, North Carolina; and printed on 60-pound Glatfelter Natural and bound by Cushing-Malloy of Ann Arbor, Michigan.